LANDING FROM AN EMIGRANT SHIP.

THEY CAME IN SHIPS

A Guide to Finding Your Immigrant
Ancestor's Arrival Record

By John Philip Colletta, Ph.D.

Ancestry

Library of Congress catalog card number
93-26835
ISBN 0-916489-42-6

First printing 1989. Revised edition 1993
10 9 8 7 6 5

For other fine products available from Ancestry, call or write:
P.O. Box 476
Salt Lake City, UT 84110-0476
1-800-ANCESTRY®
(1-800-262-3787)

Thanks, Nonna!

CONTENTS

PREFACE TO THE SECOND EDITION

They came in ships. How else could they have come here—the Europeans, the Africans, the Asians who arrived between 1565 and 1954? They came in sailing vessels and steamships to Atlantic, Pacific, Great Lakes, and Gulf Coast ports. Every ship had its passenger list or cargo manifest—and many of these records, which identify the immigrants who came, and when, and on what ship, have survived.

Thus, most Americans can discover what ship brought their ancestors to this continent. Your search may be easy and result in quick success, or it may be a challenge requiring time and persistence. Every ancestor's story is unique, so every search for an ancestor's ship is unique. By following the instructions provided in this book, however, chances are good that you will find your immigrant ancestor's name in the passenger list of the ship that brought him or her to America.

Books and articles about ship passenger lists abound, and more appear every year. Some are bibliographies of lists that have appeared in published works. Some are alphabetical indexes to the names appearing in selected published or unpublished lists. Some describe the experience of immigrating to America or discuss the sailing vessels and steamships that brought the immigrants. Some deal with particular ethnic or national groups and the specific time periods and seaports of their immigration stories. However, prior to the publication of this book, there was no manual that explained to the family researcher exactly how to use the wealth of published and unpublished materials now available to locate a particular individual named in an old ship passenger list. This book was written specifically to fill that need.

Since this volume first appeared in 1989, sustained publishing on the topic of arrival records has been supported by increasing interest on the part of the public. This country's ever-growing number of genealogists—as well as many visitors to the Ellis Island immigrant receiving center in New York—have expressed a desire for more instruction on how to search for an immigrant ancestor's ship, especially among the arrival records that are not indexed. In response to this continued publishing, therefore, and to this demand for additional instruction, this second, revised edition has been prepared. The text and bibliography have been updated and expanded extensively to reflect the latest resources available and to explain how to make the fullest use of them to find the ship passenger list that bears your ancestor's name.

A variety of records *other* than ship passenger lists may help you identify an immigrant ancestor. They deal with colonial land grants, indentured servitude, oaths of allegiance, naturalization, and other kinds of documentary evidence of new arrivals in America. These may prove especially valuable for researching an immigrant ancestor in the colonial period—for which many ship passenger lists no longer exist—and many have appeared in print. Consider, for example, this source for the colony of Virginia:

> Nugent, Nell Marion, comp. *Cavaliers and Pioneers: Abstracts of Virginia Land Patents and Grants.* Richmond, Va.: Virginia State Library. Vol. 1, 1623–66 (1934); vol. 2, 1666–95 (1977); vol. 3, 1695–1732 (1979).

And for the colony of Maryland:

> Skordas, Gust. *The Early Settlers of Maryland.* Baltimore: Genealogical Publishing Co., 1968.

And for the Delaware River Valley:

> Johnson, Amandus. *The Swedish Settlements on the Delaware, 1638–1664.* 2 vols. 1911. Reprint. Baltimore: Genealogical Publishing Co., 1969.

Also in print are emigration records of the colonial period, which document persons leaving their homelands for America. For example:

Hotten, John Camden. *The Original Lists of Persons of Quality, 1600–1700.* London: The Public Record Office, 1874. Reprint. Baltimore: Genealogical Publishing Co., 1962.

This classic work has been updated and expanded in a series of books by Peter Wilson Coldham, beginning with:

The Complete Book of Emigrants, 1607–1660. Baltimore: Genealogical Publishing Co., 1987.

These other types of arrival records and departure records, however—though they are valuable sources of information about immigrant ancestors and should not be overlooked by any family historian—name the colonial immigrant's ship only rarely. The focus of this manual, on the other hand, is *strictly* ship passenger lists. However, a ship passenger list is much more than a mere roster of names.

The introduction to this manual explains how you can extract more from a passenger list than just the name of your ancestor's ship and its date of arrival. The diverse data contained in passenger lists can be understood, interpreted, and combined with other information about your ancestors to advance and expand your genealogical knowledge and enhance your family history. The introduction to this second edition discusses new ways for you to do this. After all, you want to get all you can out of your search!

Chapter 1 prepares you to undertake the search. It tells you not only what fundamental facts you need to know about your immigrant ancestor before beginning, but it suggests where you can find that information as well. This second edition has been expanded to address the common problem of surname changes, and it discusses additional sources for obtaining the information necessary to get your search under way. To focus your efforts, an essential distinction is drawn between searching in pre-1820 and post-1820 lists.

Chapters 2 and 3 guide you step-by-step through the research process, whether your immigrant ancestor arrived in a sailing vessel in the sixteenth, seventeenth, eighteenth, or nineteenth century, or on board a steamship in the nineteenth or twentieth century. Specific strategies are suggested for sample research scenarios, and detailed instruction is given on how to use the indexes and resource materials at your disposal to overcome obstacles to your search. This second edition also contains an expanded discussion of immigration legislation as it affected the creation and content of arrival records, as well as new information about U.S. ports of entry.

Chapter 4 is new for this edition and contains substantial new material. It addresses how to search for a ship if your ancestor arrived during a year that is not included in any National Archives index. It also explores alternative resources and demonstrates how to use each one of them in a variety of sample research scenarios—when one methodology does not work, try another! And be aware that you need not go to Washington, D.C., to use the National Archives publications mentioned in this book. They are also available at the twelve National Archives regional archives located throughout the United States, as well as through the Church of Jesus Christ of Latter-day Saints Family History Library (LDS church library) in Salt Lake City, Utah.

Throughout the text of this manual the author shares with you many specific and helpful hints, warnings, and suggestions based on his years of experience researching ship passenger lists and lecturing on the subject at the National Archives in Washington, D.C. How to decipher illegible microfilm; determine your ancestor's most likely port of departure and port of arrival; use the newspapers of the port city; discover births and deaths at sea; discover how long it took a sailing ship or a steamship to cross the Atlantic; learn whether your ancestor was a stowaway or a member of the ship's crew; obtain a picture of your ancestor's vessel—these are just a few of the numerous issues addressed based on the author's personal experience. Any of this information, at some point in your search, may be indispensable to locating your ancestor's ship.

The conclusion of this second edition provides an expanded chronology of Ellis Island. Though millions of Americans are descended from immigrants who arrived at New York, not all of those immigrants passed through Ellis Island. The conclusion shows how Ellis Island relates to the history of the port of New York, and it helps you to understand your ancestor's immigration story.

Following the text is a select bibliography—updated and expanded for this second edition to include more than sixty works— because undertaking the search for your ancestor's ship requires a familiarity with the available resources. The annotations in the bibliography help you determine at a glance whether any particular work may be useful in your search.

This manual closes with a chart titled "How to Find Your Immigrant Ancestor's Ship." This chart was prepared by the author for the National Park Service as a part of the Ellis Island exhibit "The Peopling of America: Four Hundred Years of Immigration History." The chart summarizes the research strategies presented in the text, allowing you to focus immediately on the method most appropriate to your search.

For it is *your* search—your journey to knowledge of your family's genesis in the New World. It is a quest that yields personal satisfaction, knowledge, and joy. Here's how you do it. . . .

INTRODUCTION

WHAT PASSENGER LISTS TELL YOU ABOUT YOUR ANCESTORS

With the founding of Saint Augustine, Florida, in 1565, Europeans began to settle *permanently* in the New World. Henceforth ships would bring not only explorers and soldiers and traders and seasonal fishermen—as they had already been doing for some decades—but entire families of men, women, and children who intended to spend the rest of their lives in North America. For this reason, 1565 is a logical beginning date for a manual on finding an ancestor's ship.

The closing of Ellis Island in 1954 provides a logical ending date. After 1954 most immigrants would travel to North America not in ships but in airplanes—though a steady trickle of arrivals by sea continues to this day.

Generally, for each voyage that a ship made to America between 1565 and 1954, a passenger list was compiled. The list is usually headed with the name of the ship, the captain's name, the port and date of the ship's departure, and the port and date of its arrival in America. Beneath this heading is a roster of the passengers on board. Almost all lists, however, include some personal information about each passenger besides his or her name. Exactly what other information was included has varied widely over the past four hundred years, as this manual will demonstrate in detail in Chapters 2 and 3.

Lists composed prior to 1893, especially those of the colonial period, may appear at first glance to be disappointingly sparse in informational content. After that date, in compliance with U.S. law, they contain an increasing amount of personal and family data about each passenger. When the few facts given in an early list, or the more plentiful data supplied in a later list, are examined and evaluated within the larger context of history, and in light of your previous genealogical findings, they add up to much more family information than the bare statistics themselves. Before examining the content of ship passenger lists in detail, therefore, it may be useful to consider this preliminary question: What can I expect to learn about my family from ship passenger lists? The answer is: more than you think—as long as you know what to look for!

Below, to alert you to the kinds of questions you should have in mind as you conduct your search, is a sampling of just three ways in which passenger lists may determine the direction of your genealogical research and add colorful breadth to your ancestor's immigration story.

BIOGRAPHICAL AND GENEALOGICAL INFORMATION

Ship passenger lists may add rich biographical and genealogical details to your family history. For example, you may discover that your ancestor sailed to the American colonies with a royal governor or other prominent personage of the period—perhaps Benjamin Franklin or Thomas Jefferson, both of whom made many transatlantic crossings. Perhaps your ancestor crossed the Pacific from China at the age of fourteen—unaccompanied. Possibly your ancestor was a stowaway, or born at sea, or one of a group of young ladies sent to America as prospective wives for unmarried settlers. All kinds of details about your ancestor's life, and the world in which he or she lived, may come to light from the passenger list.

I discovered from ship lists of 1898 and 1902, for example, that a great-great-grandmother's third husband and then fourth husband—both of whom I knew were born and died in Sicily—had crossed the Atlantic and spent time in New York City with their children from previous marriages. This information dramatized the surprising mobility that even a poor family from a tiny Sicilian village enjoyed at the turn of the century. It showed how families separated by an ocean were able to keep in touch, thanks to the wondrous advances made by steam-powered transportation.

If your ancestors from southern or eastern Europe emigrated after 1921, you may discover that they booked passage to America on French steamships leaving from Le Havre rather than on vessels leaving from ports closer to home. Ship lists reveal that many southern and eastern Europeans devised schemes to circumvent the immigration restrictions imposed by the Emergency Quota Act of 1921 (see Chapter 4). They were desperate to be reunited with husbands, wives, or children already established in the United States.

THE OVERSEAS LINK

Ship passenger lists may supply the vital transatlantic link you need to pursue your research overseas. You may find, for instance, that an ancestor with an English surname sailed from Glasgow, Scotland. This unexpected revelation would lead you to explore whether and when your ancestor's family had moved from England to Scotland, and would enable you to pursue your research in a country you might never have imagined. Or a French Huguenot ancestor may appear in the passenger list of a Dutch ship out of Amsterdam, providing the clue you need to continue your research on that family in the Netherlands before progressing back to France.

My grandmother told me her mother had been born in the Sicilian town of Bagheria, but I was unable to discover a birth record for her there. Then I found her name in the passenger list of the ship that brought her to America and discovered that she had *not* been born in Bagheria, as my grandmother had always believed, but in the village of Castronovo. Writing a letter to the Catholic parish in Castronovo secured my great-grandmother's baptismal record and allowed me to continue to research her ancestry in that village.

THE MIGRATION STORY

The facts of your immigrant ancestor's life and voyage take on fuller meaning when viewed within the context of his or her family. You may be able to deduce from the names included on the ship passenger list whether your ancestor was traveling alone or in the company of family members. Which brothers or sisters also came? Which ones stayed in the Old Country? Did your ancestor's entire extended family eventually immigrate—including cousins, uncles, and aunts? Did some relatives go back? Who? And why?

Your ancestor might have been the adventurous trailblazer, the one who led the way for the rest of his family to follow. Or your ancestor may have been the last to come, the one reluctant to give up the land and culture of birth until necessity imposed the decision. Ship lists reveal how your ancestor fit into the migration story of his family, and how the migration story of your family fits into the larger saga of the building of America.

The list of the ship *Nile*, which entered New York from Le Havre in 1830, taught me that a fifty-one-year-old ancestor of mine had traveled to the United States not only with all of his own children, their spouses, and *their* children, but with all of his families-in-law as well! They had all been residents of the same village of Lorraine, France, and they had evidently chosen to lighten the burdens and risks of crossing the Atlantic in a small sailing vessel by sharing those burdens and risks—under the leadership of their elderly *pater familias*, my ancestor.

With the age of steam, young men from Europe were able to travel to the United States and home again annually to satisfy this country's seasonal demand for labor. They came in the spring and left before winter, earning the sobriquet "birds of passage." By their second or third voyage, many of these workers were bringing their wives and children with them to settle in the United States. Some families went back and forth across the Atlantic a number of times before remaining here for good. Passenger lists help establish not only the composition of these families—which children were born where and when—but also a chronology of their travels and a fuller understanding of what immigrating meant to them.

Biographical and genealogical information, the transatlantic link, and your family's migration story represent just a sampling of the numerous ways in which information from ship passenger lists can help you expand your research activities and your knowledge of your family's history. So how do you get to that passenger list? . . .

CHAPTER 1

WHAT YOU NEED TO KNOW AND WHERE TO FIND IT

B efore beginning your search, you should be aware of what facts you need to know and where to find them.

FIRST YOU MUST KNOW THE PASSENGER'S . . .

FULL, ORIGINAL NAME

You must know your immigrant ancestor's full, original name—given name as well as surname. Discovering this may present a challenge because many American families do not go by the same family name that their immigrant ancestor did. You may spell your name in a slightly different way; it might be an anglicized or shortened version or a transliteration of the original; or your surname may be a literal English translation of your ancestor's name. The historical vagaries that caused surnames to change are multifarious, and you are far from alone if your family name is not the same as your immigrant ancestor's. Nevertheless, whatever your personal story may be, you must learn your immigrant ancestor's full name as it was used in the Old Country before you can begin your search.

This information is necessary because passenger lists were prepared in the port of embarkation before the ship sailed. Beginning in 1820 the blank lists were printed and sold to ship companies by private printers in the United States. From 1891 onward the U.S. government printed the blank lists and provided them to the ship companies, which distributed them to their respective ports in

Europe to be completed for each voyage, normally by the ship's purser. As a result, the printed column headings are in English, but the names appear as the ship's purser penned them on the list.

Though some pursers may have transcribed each passenger's name from passports or travel papers or other identification, it appears that often—before the twentieth century, at least—pursers simply asked the passengers their names and wrote them on the list as they *sounded*. The errors that resulted from this practice were inevitable, especially with surnames transliterated from non-Latin alphabets, such as Russian, Ukrainian, Chinese, and Japanese. Take, for example, a Jewish tailor from Kiev, in the Ukraine, who is leaving from Bremen, Germany, on a ship of the North German Lloyd Line around 1905 (as thousands did). Though he is un-schooled, he can recognize and perhaps even sign his own name, but only in the Cyrillic alphabet, or perhaps in Hebrew. He has no familiarity whatsoever with the Latin alphabet. When the tailor tells his name to the German purser filling out the passenger list, the official immediately transliterates the name (writes it in Latin let-ters)—as he hears and understands it. Naturally, the Jewish emigrant is unable to correct the purser's transliteration if it is not correct. This explains why three brothers coming from the Ukraine on three different ships might end up using three variants of their family name.

Even surnames and given names from languages that use the Latin alphabet were sometimes corrupted on passenger lists. For instance, many ships of American and British lines embarked from the port of Le Havre, France. The purser was normally an American or Englishman whose work and travels had provided him with a rudimentary knowledge of French and German. When hearing and writing down the names of French and German passengers, there-fore, the purser might translate into English a name whose meaning he knew—turning *Pierre* into *Peter*, for example, or *Schmidt* into *Smith*; or, worse yet, translating the French *La Fontaine* to *Fountain* or the German *Vogel* to *Bird*; or dropping the umlaut from *Müller* and writing down *Mueller*, *Miller*, or just *Muller*. The official might simply do the best he can to spell unfamiliar names as he hears them—and French, if not German, is a distinctly unphonetic language. Unschooled French and German emigrants were unable to correct the purser's transcription of their names.

When searching for an immigrant ancestor's ship, therefore, always bear in mind a few possible variant spellings of the surname. You may need all of them to find your ancestor! If your ancestor habitually used a nickname, make note of that, too; he will be listed under the nickname if that is the name he told the purser.

It is important to remember that women in some European countries, such as France and Italy (though not Germany), conduct matters of record under their maiden names. Therefore, they are listed in nineteenth- and twentieth-century passenger lists under their maiden names, even though they may be married and even though they may be traveling with their husbands or children. In lists of the colonial period, however, you will find them using their husband's surname.

If you suspect your ancestor was traveling in the company of a relative or neighbor, note the surname of the relative or neighbor. The traveling partner's name could be crucial to finding your own ancestor, as Chapter 3 will explain.

APPROXIMATE AGE AT ARRIVAL

You must know the approximate age of your immigrant ancestor at the time he or she arrived. This information is necessary to distinguish him or her from other immigrants with the same name. Not hundreds, not thousands, but *millions* of immigrants came to America between 1565 and 1954; thus, when searching ship passenger lists, you may discover that a name you thought was unique, or at least rare, was actually very common. Many ethnic and national groups around the world observed rigid traditions for naming their children; generation after generation, the same names reappear. No name is so uncommon that you may disregard this requirement!

APPROXIMATE DATE OF ARRIVAL

To know where to begin your search, you must know the approximate date of your ancestor's arrival at the U.S. port. If you can learn the year and perhaps the season of the year or the specific month, you are prepared to begin your search. Even knowing only an approximate year may be sufficient. However, the closer you can get to an actual date—month, day, year—the better.

WHERE CAN YOU FIND THIS INFORMATION?

There is no point in searching for your immigrant ancestor's ship until you have a good idea of these three facts: your ancestor's name, age at arrival, and date of arrival. How can you discover them?

ORAL FAMILY TRADITION

Has a story about your immigrant ancestor been passed down from generation to generation within your family—perhaps including the name of the ship? Was your ancestor a member of the crew who "jumped ship" when the vessel arrived at the U.S. port? Did your ancestor from the sunny Mediterranean Basin arrive in snow-covered Boston with no winter clothing? Did your Scandinavian ancestor arrive at Baltimore on a sweltering August afternoon with only heavy woolen clothing to wear? Perhaps your ancestor arrived in America on Christmas day or the Fourth of July. Or was your ancestor's ship detained in quarantine because a case of cholera had been discovered on board? Possibly your ancestor entered New York in the late nineteenth century but did not pass through Ellis Island, as you may have assumed. . . .

No matter how farfetched family lore may sound, it always holds a kernel of truth—and that kernel of truth, however small, could provide the essential clue that leads you to your ancestor's ship. No matter how insignificant the details of the oral tradition may seem, one of those details could be the hint that rewards your search with success—so take note of *every* family tradition you hear!

PERSONAL AND FAMILY DOCUMENTS

Personal and family documents may yield one or all of the three essential facts you need. These types of documents include passports and travel papers, family letters, diaries, Bible inscriptions, death announcements and remembrance cards, newspaper obituaries, wedding invitations and birth and christening announcements, steamship ticket stubs and Ellis Island Inspection Cards, citizenship class diplomas, and other similar documents.

If your family has been in the United States for only two or three generations, you might find such keepsakes in the attic or basement of your parents' home, or in the possession of a relative. Even old family photographs that have been labeled by a thoughtful great aunt or uncle may provide the information you seek. If your family immigrated in the early seventeenth century, you may still be able to discover some treasured document about the immigrant ancestor. When interviewing relatives about your family's origins in America, be sure to ask: Who has the family photos . . . an heirloom from the Old Country . . . family documents? Contact that relative immediately!

CIVIL AND CHURCH RECORDS

Civil records of birth, marriage, and death, probate records, and military service records may be found in archives, courthouses, and libraries around the United States. In addition, churches have records of baptisms, marriages, and burials. Tombstone inscriptions, too, can be useful. Any one of these resources, or a combination of them, may give you the three essential facts you seek.

Federal censuses may be helpful, especially if your immigrant ancestor was living in the United States in 1900, 1910, or 1920. In those years the census takers asked foreign-born residents what year they came to the United States, how many years they had resided here, and what their citizenship status was. Federal censuses are available at the National Archives in Washington, D.C., the twelve regional archives, and numerous libraries, including the LDS church Family History Library. The 1900 and 1920 censuses are fully indexed—the 1900 census by individual name, the 1920 census by head of household and unrelated individuals; but the 1910 census is indexed for only twenty-one states.

State censuses may provide the same information for an earlier period. Facts about a foreign-born resident's year of immigration and citizenship status appear on many nineteenth-century state censuses long before they appear on federal censuses. To cite but one example, the 1855 New York State Census contains such data. State censuses are available in your state archives, library, or historical society and in many local libraries, too.

If your ancestor became a U.S. citizen, the record of his naturalization may contain the facts you need to find his ship. This record may include not only the year he immigrated and his age at that time, but the name of the ship and the port and date of arrival as well. The amount and type of information given in naturalization records varies widely, however. Naturalization records made in federal courts are available either at the National Archives or one of its twelve regional archives. Naturalizations made in state courts are found in county courthouses, and naturalizations made in municipal courts are generally preserved at the city hall.

If your immigrant ancestor, after being naturalized, applied to the U.S. State Department for a passport, the passport application will contain the facts about his immigration and naturalization. Since passports were not required by law until 1941 (except for a few brief periods during wars), most Americans did not bother to apply for one. Many others, however, did, including naturalized citizens returning to their homelands to visit relatives. Passport applications from 1791 through 1925 are available at the National Archives, and there are registers and indexes to them.

Finally, if your immigrant ancestor took advantage of the Homestead Act of 1862 to obtain free land from the U.S. government, his homestead file will contain information about his immigration and naturalization. Homestead files are kept in the National Archives building at the National Federal Records Center in Suitland,

Maryland, and may be accessed by using the legal description of your ancestor's land.

PUBLISHED GENEALOGIES AND LOCAL HISTORIES

There are thousands of published genealogies and local histories from which you might obtain your immigrant ancestor's name, age at arrival, and date of arrival. These works cover geographic areas all over the United States and time periods from the sixteenth through the twentieth centuries. New ones are being published and old ones are being reprinted.

Also numerous and growing in number and diversity are histories that chronicle the appearance and growth of ethnic and national groups in the United States. For example, if your ancestor was from Bohemia, there are, among others:

> Rosicky, Rose, comp. *A History of the Czechs (Bohemians) in Nebraska.* Omaha, Nebr.: Czech Historical Society of Nebraska, 1929. Reprint. Evanston, Ind.: Unigraphic, 1977.

> Benes, Frank. *Czechs in Manitowoc County, Wisconsin, 1847– 1932.* Manitowoc, Wis.: Manitowoc County Historical Society, 1979. .

Consult a manual on genealogy for more details concerning oral family tradition, personal and family documents, civil and church records, and published genealogies and local histories, and to learn whether other resources might exist that supply the three facts you seek. Books on genealogical sources and methods are numerous and provide information about where records are held, what information they contain, and how to gain access to them. The bibliography at the end of this manual lists several such how-to and reference books. You *can* come up with the facts you need to find your immigrant ancestor in the ship passenger lists.

THE TWO MAJOR PERIODS OF SHIP PASSENGER LISTS

Ship passenger lists are divided into two groups: those earlier than 1820 and those of 1820 and later. How you search will be determined by whether your ancestor arrived before or after 1820.

1565–1819

If your ancestor arrived between 1565 and 1819, the original passenger list, if it still exists, might be in any archive, museum, courthouse, basement, or attic. Lists of this early period are not preserved in the National Archives. In fact, there is no central depository of any kind where these old lists are gathered together and preserved, and the vast majority of them have long ago disappeared. But many *have* been published! Search in the library in indexes to *published* lists.

1820–1954

If your ancestor arrived between 1820 and 1954, a microfilm copy of the passenger list probably exists in the National Archives. Search in the indexes there or, if they are not helpful, in the alternative resources described in Chapter 4.

Whether you are searching for a pre-1820 list that has been published or a post-1820 list on microfilm at the National Archives, your method will involve two steps: 1) examine any index to passenger arrival records that may contain the name of your ancestor; 2) use the information given in that index to locate the passenger list. The list may exist either in published form in the library or on microfilm at the National Archives.

Note that the indexes you use are not physically attached to the passenger lists they index. They are separate, having been prepared many years after the creation of the lists by compilers and bibliographers to help researchers like you find a particular passenger. This means you may perform the first step of your search in one place and then have to travel (or write) to another place to perform the second step.

Now you have the fundamental facts you need to begin the search for your immigrant ancestor's ship. You know your ancestor's full, original name, approximate age at arrival, and approximate date of arrival, and you know whether your search will be in pre-1820 or post-1820 ship passenger lists—so on with the search. . . .

CHAPTER 2

PASSENGER LISTS OF 1565-1819

Prior to 1820 there was no federal law requiring the recording of passenger arrival information in the United States. This explains why there are no passenger lists dated earlier than 1820 in the National Archives (with the minor exceptions noted in Chapter 3). Immigration matters were handled wherever immigrants arrived, first by the individual colonies, later by the states, and sometimes by the port cities themselves. Any records of incoming passengers considered necessary were maintained locally. Whatever pre-1820 ship lists and records of passenger arrivals that may have existed, therefore, have long since been lost, destroyed, or scattered into libraries, historical societies, museums, archives, and private hands all over the United States. (The Pennsylvania State Archives, for instance, holds captains' lists from 1727 through 1808 for the port of Philadelphia. This collection, however, is a very happy and atypical instance.)

Because they were maintained locally, pre-1820 ship passenger lists vary broadly in the amount and type of information they contain. They typically provide the ship's name and the name of the captain; the date and port of embarkation or the date and port of arrival, or both; and the name of each passenger on board—though members of a family traveling with the head of household are not always named individually but accounted for rather as, for instance, "with his wife," or "with wife and two children." The age of each passenger was also commonly given, as well as each one's country of origin, occupation, and sometimes the number of bags each was carrying.

There is no comprehensive catalog or index to extant pre-1820 ship passenger lists. However, many of these early lists have been published over the years—in state histories, local histories, historical society quarterlies, genealogical books and articles, scholarly studies about colonial America and immigration, and the like. To find your immigrant ancestor's ship in this period, therefore, you must rely entirely on indexes to published passenger lists. You must discover whether the list containing your ancestor's name has ever appeared in published form and, if it has, where and when so that you can obtain and examine it.

INDEXES TO PUBLISHED ARRIVAL LISTS

Armed with your ancestor's full, original name, approximate age at arrival, and approximate date of arrival, you are ready to charge into the library and attack the indexes to ship passenger lists. The bibliography at the end of this manual contains a wide selection of such indexes. Each index, however, is different, having been compiled according to the specific criteria set by the individual compiler. Each index covers only a particular port or ports, a particular time period, or a particular ethnic, religious, or otherwise identifiable group. Therefore, before you use any index to passenger arrival records, read the introductory material in the front of the volume carefully to understand precisely *what* is indexed in that volume and *how* it is indexed. Titles can be deceiving! To help you decide which indexes might be helpful to your personal search, the bibliography includes annotations that summarize what each work covers and how they differ from one another.

The first step to finding your immigrant ancestor's ship, therefore, is to search these indexes for your ancestor's name. If you are lucky enough to know an additional fact or two about your ancestor—perhaps nationality or port of arrival, or that your ancestor was a member of an identifiable group (such as indentured servants), or where your immigrant ancestor first settled in the United States—you can bypass many of these indexes and focus exclusively on the indexes compiled for that particular nationality, port, group, or place. The best research strategy is the one that makes fullest use of your knowledge and saves you the most time and effort.

Below are four sample research scenarios that demonstrate how to use indexes to published ship passenger lists based on what you already know, or do not know, about your ancestor's immigration story. For each scenario, the title of a major work is provided to suggest the kind of index you would consult in that particular research situation. For complete publication data on all titles, refer to the bibliography. Neither the bibliography, however, nor the following examples are by any means exhaustive. They are illustrative only. You have to do your own research!

IF ALL YOU KNOW ARE THE THREE BASIC FACTS

Search for your ancestor's name in *any* index to published arrival records, such as this, the most extensive one available:

> Filby, P. William, with Mary K. Meyer, eds. *Passenger and Immigration Lists Index: A Guide to Published Arrival Records of More Than 1,775,000 Passengers Who Came to the New World between the Sixteenth and the Early Twentieth Centuries.*

IF YOU ALSO KNOW YOUR ANCESTOR'S NATIONALITY

Search for your ancestor's name in indexes to published arrival records compiled by nationality, such as:

> Yoder, Don, ed. *Pennsylvania German Immigrants, 1709-1786: Lists Consolidated from Yearbooks of The Pennsylvania German Folklore Society.*

IF YOU ALSO KNOW YOUR ANCESTOR'S "GROUP" OR PLACE OF SETTLEMENT

Search for your ancestor's name in indexes to published arrival records compiled by religious or otherwise identifiable group or by geographic place of settlement, such as:

Tepper, Michael H., ed. *Emigrants to Pennsylvania, 1641–1819: A Consolidation of Ship Passenger Lists from the Pennsylvania Magazine of History and Biography.*

IF YOU ALSO KNOW YOUR ANCESTOR'S PORT OF ARRIVAL

Search for your ancestor's name in indexes to published arrival records that are compiled by port of arrival, such as:

Strassburger, Ralph Beaver, comp. *Pennsylvania German Pioneers: A Publication of the Original Lists of Arrivals in the Port of Philadelphia from 1727 to 1808.*

When you find your ancestor's name in any of these indexes, you have completed step one of your search. Proceed to step two: use the reference cited in the index to locate the published list. The index will indicate in what journal, book, or article the passenger list has been published. It will provide a title, author, and any other information necessary for you to identify the published work. Write down this descriptive information and find a library that has a copy of the work.

Once you have the published work in hand, turn to the passenger list and read it line by line to find your ancestor's name. When you come to the name, be certain you have found *your* ancestor—and not someone else's of the same name—by double-checking the data you find in the published ship list against what you already know to be your ancestor's full, original name, approximate age at arrival, and approximate date of arrival. If they coincide, you have *probably* found your ancestor's ship.

Finally, to *confirm* that you have found your ancestor's ship, you must bring to bear a corroborating fact—some piece of evidence about your immigrant ancestor found in the list itself or in some other source. Say, for example, that you know your ancestor, Andrew Smith, had a son, James, and the Andrew Smith you find in the list is enumerated with a wife and a son—James. Or you know your ancestor, Daniel O'Shea, came to America with his brother, Patrick, and the Daniel O'Shea you find in the list is enumerated beside a Patrick O'Shea. The enormous number of immigrants with the same or similar names, and the scant information provided about each passenger in the old ship lists, requires that you confirm your finding by applying at least one such corroborating fact.

Let us say, for example, that you are looking for the ship that brought your immigrant ancestor, William Bechet. The earliest record you have found of William Bechet in America is a Louisiana census of 1721, in which he appears with a wife and children. His age is recorded as twenty-seven, and you hypothesize that he came within a few years of that census. Searching through Filby's *Passenger and Immigration Lists Index* (see bibliography), you find no Bechets at all in the original three-volume set or the 1982 through 1985 cumulative supplement; but in the 1986 through 1990 cumulative supplement you find:

Bechet, Guillaume; Louisiana, 1719 8421 p453

With wife

This looks promising. "Guillaume" is French for William, and all evidence indicates that your ancestor was French. Checking the Sources Index in the front of the volume, you note that source 8421 is: "Ship Lists of Passengers Leaving France for Louisiana, 1718-1724," translated by Albert Laplace Dart, in *The Louisiana Historical Quarterly*, volume 15 number 1 (January 1932), pages 68 through 77; and volume 15 number 3 (July 1932), pages 453 through 467.

Visiting a library that has back issues of *The Louisiana Historical Quarterly*, you find volume fifteen and turn to page 453. There is the article, and the first ship list transcribed and translated is that of the flute *The Marie*, which sailed from France on May 28, 1719. The list includes one "Guillaume Bechet," "sa femme" (his wife) and "Jean Bechet agé de 4 ans" (John Bechet, four years old). Though no age is given for Guillaume or his wife, and their relationship to the four-year-old boy is not indicated, the three passengers are grouped together; that is sufficient to confirm that you have found your ancestor because you know that your William Bechet had a son, John, who was born about 1715.

This particular list might more aptly be called a record of departure from France rather than a record of arrival in America.

But in this case it serves the same purpose, since you know the flute did reach Louisiana. Given the sailing date of May 28, 1719, your ancestors would most likely have arrived between late June and late August. (For more about "emigration lists," see Chapter 4.)

Your own research scenario may lead you to follow through on one, two, three, or all four of these sample strategies or perhaps some combination of them. You may find it necessary to devise yet another strategy appropriate to your own research situation. Your course of action will depend on how much you know—or do not know—about the facts of your ancestor's immigration. Every piece you can fit into the puzzle will help complete the picture. Finding your immigrant ancestor's ship in this early period—1565 to 1819— often requires creative research methods. A little luck does not hurt either!

BIBLIOGRAPHY OF PUBLISHED SHIP PASSENGER LISTS

If you happen to know the name of your ancestor's ship, you may not need to consult any of the indexes described above. Instead, you may turn immediately to a bibliography of published arrival records and look for your ancestor's ship. For although—as noted above— there is no comprehensive catalog or index to *extant* pre-1820 ship passenger lists, there *is* an extensive bibliography of passenger arrival records that have appeared in *published* works:

> Filby, P. William. *Passenger and Immigration Lists Bibliography, 1538–1900: Being a Guide to Published Lists of Arrivals in the United States and Canada.*

This work lists hundreds of publications in which passenger arrival lists have appeared. Using the index in the back of the book, search for publications likely to contain your ancestor's ship list—that is, select works about your ancestor's place of arrival or place of settlement or about your ancestor's ethnic, national, or religious group. Read the compiler's notes about each of those works to see which ships are named in them. If your ancestor's ship is mentioned, note whether the date of arrival coincides with your ancestor's approximate date of arrival. If it does not, the list is evidently from another crossing made by that ship, not your ancestor's crossing. If the date does coincide, however, locate the source cited, find the list in it, and search the list line by line for your ancestor's name. When you find it, be sure to apply some corroborating piece of evidence to be sure you have found your ancestor and not someone else's!

For example, if you had known that your ancestor, William Bechet, arrived on the flute *The Marie*, you could have learned from Filby's *Passenger and Immigration Lists Bibliography* that at least one list from that vessel had been published—for a crossing made to Louisiana in 1719—in *The Louisiana Historical Quarterly* of 1932. That would have provided sufficient incentive for you to locate the issue and find your ancestor's name in the list.

IF YOUR ANCESTOR WAS A SLAVE

If your immigrant ancestor was a slave, finding the ship that brought him or her to America will require a methodology completely distinct from the one outlined above. Slaves were not listed by name in any passenger list. Rather, they were logged in the slave ship's manifest as cargo, usually in age and sex categories. On occasion, slave manifests were more detailed, but usually only when ships were transporting slaves between domestic ports. Therefore, it is rarely possible to state categorically that you have found the ship on which your enslaved ancestor was brought to America.

Nevertheless, circumstantial evidence of your ancestor's ship *may* be obtained if you know where, when, and by whom the slave was first purchased, and then search through records pertaining to that place and time and slaveholder. Finding them is not an easy task because such records could be housed almost anywhere. Here are a few sample repositories:

NATIONAL ARCHIVES

The National Archives has manifests of some ships that imported slaves into the ports of Savannah, Georgia; Mobile, Alabama; and New Orleans during the period 1789 through 1808. They are part of Record Group 36 (Records of the U.S. Customs Service) and may be examined in Washington, D.C. Since they contain no names, these lists have no index.

MUSEUMS

There are museums around the country that house special collections that include manifests of slave ships and private papers of slave owners. For example, the Peabody Museum of Salem, Massachusetts, has some slave ship logbooks.

LIBRARIES

Some libraries have published compilations of documents relating to the slave trade in America. These include official correspondence, proceedings, and reports of the officers of the shipping companies. One major work in this field is:

> Donnan, Elizabeth, ed. *Documents Illustrative of the History of the Slave Trade in America.* 4 vols. Washington, D.C.: Carnegie Institution of Washington, 1930–35. Reprint. New York: Octagon Books, 1965.

For a list of archives, museums, and libraries that house major collections of value to African American genealogy, see:

> Cerny, Johni. "Black Ancestral Research." Chapter 19 in *The Source, A Guidebook of American Genealogy.* Salt Lake City: Ancestry, 1984.

Certainly not to be overlooked in searching for the ship of a slave ancestor is oral tradition, so valued and reliable in African American families.

LEARNING MORE ABOUT YOUR ANCESTOR'S SHIP

Once you discover the name of the ship that brought your ancestor to America, you will notice that it is preceded by the term "ship," "bark," "flute," "sloop," "snow," "brig," or some other designation. This term—which indicates the vessel's rig (how many masts and sails it had)—tells you what kind of vessel it was.

Libraries frequently contain many illustrated books devoted to ships, so it is usually not difficult to learn more about the type of vessel your ancestor traveled in or to obtain a reproduction of a drawing, painting, engraving, or lithograph of it. Simply find a picture of a ship, bark, flute, or whatever other type of vessel your ancestor sailed in, that corresponds to the era in which your ancestor crossed the ocean. Note the rig of such a ship, its weight, how many passengers it carried, and so forth to better understand your ancestor's immigration story. (The bibliography at the end of this manual includes several books about crossing the Atlantic by sailing vessel.)

In addition, museums specializing in maritime history may be helpful in supplying a picture of, and information about, the vessel in which your ancestor sailed. (See Chapter 4, "Obtaining a Picture of Your Ancestor's Ship," for more about these museums.)

CHAPTER 3

PASSENGER LISTS OF 1820-1954

In 1819, Congress passed an act that required captains of vessels arriving at U.S. ports from foreign countries to submit a list of passengers to the Collector of Customs at the port of entry. This act was signed into law and went into effect on January 1, 1820. This explains why the thousands of passenger lists at the National Archives are all (with the few exceptions noted below) post-1819. These lists are divided into two groups: Customs Passenger Lists (1820 through ca. 1891) and Immigration Passenger Lists (1891 through 1954).

CUSTOMS PASSENGER LISTS (1820-ca. 1891)

Passenger lists dating from 1820 to about 1891 are called Customs Passenger Lists because collecting them was the responsibility of the Bureau of Customs. The law stipulated that the list contain the names of the ship and its master, its port of embarkation, and the date and port of its arrival; and each passenger's name, age, sex, occupation, and nationality (see illustration). No more information than this was required on Customs Passenger Lists, so many of these lists have only five columns. Often, though, a sixth column was used to record each passenger's berth number or the number of pieces of baggage each passenger was carrying, or to note deaths occurring at sea. Therefore, to be certain you have found your ancestor in these lists, you may need some corroborating evidence from other documents pertaining to your immigrant ancestor.

Customs Passenger Lists (part of Record Group 36, Records of the U.S. Customs Service) exist for the major ports of Baltimore,

Customs Passenger List. This sample is from National Archives microfilm M425, *Passenger Lists of Vessels Arriving at Philadelphia, 1800–1882*, roll 53, Jan. 2–Dec. 24, 1838. It is the list of the bark *Fairfield*, arrived July 17, 1838, and it shows Robert Ellis and his family on lines 75 through 80.

Boston, New Orleans, New York, and Philadelphia as well as for numerous minor Atlantic, Gulf Coast, and Great Lakes ports.

How many American ports did immigrants use? In colonial times immigrants landed at hundreds of places along the rivers flowing into the Atlantic Ocean and Gulf of Mexico. No "immigrant receiving stations" enforced any physical, mental, or financial requirements for admission. As already noted, each colony or port city exercised authority over its own immigration affairs. The major port of entry during the eighteenth century was Philadelphia. With continued and increased immigration, however, certain ports gradually became established points of arrival, and states assumed control of regulating immigration matters.

Throughout the nineteenth century and into the early twentieth century, a total of 101 ports were used. (For a complete, state-by-state listing of these ports along with an account of the ship passenger lists that exist for each one, the years the lists cover, and their indexes, see Chapter 2 of *Guide to Genealogical Research in the National Archives*.) By the 1840s, New York City had surpassed Philadelphia as the busiest port of entry.

It was during the 1840s that shipping companies started to realize the profits to be made in the transporting of immigrants; all kinds of abuses developed, the worst of which was overcrowding. To alleviate overcrowding, Congress passed a series of laws establishing tonnage-to-passenger ratios for ships arriving at U.S. ports.

In 1875, Congress asserted its prerogative to legislate immigration affairs by passing a law forbidding admission into the United States of criminals and women "brought for lewd and immoral purposes." The law was challenged and the case went all the way to the Supreme Court, which upheld the federal government's jurisdiction over immigration matters. From 1875, therefore, the reception of immigrants arriving at all U.S. ports was handled jointly by federal and state officials. Though this shared federal/state system engendered tension and disputes, it lasted for fifteen years.

In 1882, Congress passed a law excluding from entry "any convict, lunatic, idiot or any person unable to take care of himself or herself without becoming a public charge." That same year, with passage of the Chinese Exclusion Act, Congress barred—for the first time in American history—a particular national group from entering the country. (Certain categories of Chinese, such as students and businessmen, continued to be admitted. For related information, see "Lists of Chinese Passengers" in Chapter 4.)

In 1890, the Secretary of the Treasury terminated the contract that his department held with the New York State Commissioners of Emigration, and the federal government assumed total control of immigration at the port of New York. The following year the joint federal/state system was terminated in all other U.S. ports. The 1891 law also provided for the creation of immigrant receiving stations at U.S. ports, and it stipulated that steamship companies would be responsible for carrying back to their homelands all passengers refused admittance by federal government inspectors at the receiving stations.

For the first time in American history, a separate bureau with its own head was created for handling immigration affairs. This was the Bureau of Immigration, created in the Department of the Treasury; its head was called the Superintendent of Immigration.

IMMIGRATION PASSENGER LISTS (1891–1954)

Passenger lists dating from 1891 to 1954 are called Immigration Passenger Lists since immigration affairs had become separate from customs matters. Standard forms for recording the required information about passengers arriving in the United States soon came into use. They were printed by the U.S. government and distributed to the steamship companies, which transported them to their respective ports of embarkation around the world to be filled in by their pursers. Responsibility for collecting and maintaining the completed lists shifted over many years from the Department of the Treasury to the Department of Commerce and Labor and then to the Department of Justice. By 1906, responsibility rested finally with the newly created Immigration and Naturalization Service.

The amount of information about each passenger required in an Immigration Passenger List expanded dramatically in the late nineteenth and early twentieth centuries (see illustration). While the vast majority of immigrants arriving prior to 1882 had come from northern and western Europe and had been predominantly Protestant, by 1907 three out of four immigrants were Catholics and Jews from southern and eastern Europe. The U.S. government wanted to know more about these millions of "New Immigrants" flocking to its shores so that Congress could effectively legislate immigration matters. Below is a summary of the data that Congress required for each passenger over the years.

1893

In 1893, the number of columns was increased from the five or six of the Customs Passenger Lists to twenty-one. In addition to each passenger's name, age, sex, occupation, and nationality, they include:

- marital status
- last residence
- final destination in the United States
- if ever in the United States before, when, where, and for how long
- if going to join a relative, the relative's name, address, and relationship
- whether able to read and write
- whether in possession of a train ticket to his or her final destination
- who paid the passage
- amount of money the passenger was carrying
- whether the passenger had ever been in a prison, almshouse, or institution for the insane, or was a polygamist
- state of health

SALOON, CABIN, AND STEERAGE ALIENS MUST BE COMPLETELY MANIFESTED.

LIST OR MANIFEST OF ALIEN PASSENGERS FOR THE UNITED

Required by the regulations of the Secretary of Commerce and Labor of the United States, under Act of Congress approved February 20, 1907, to be delivered

S. S. FLORIDA   sailing from   April 5 1908   , 190

Immigration Passenger List. This list is from National Archives microfilm T715, *Passenger and Crew Lists of Vessels Arriving at New York 1897–1957*, roll 1095, "Volumes 2404–2405, April 20, 1908." It is the list of the S.S. *Florida*, arrived April 20, 1908, and it shows Salvatore Piraino on line 15.

STATES IMMIGRATION OFFICER AT PORT OF ARRIVAL.

THIS SHEET IS FOR STEERAGE PASSENGERS.

List 22

598

to the United States Immigration Officer by the Commanding Officer of any vessel having such passengers on board upon arrival at a port in the United States.

Arriving at Port of NEW-YORK _____ , 190_

Immigration Passenger List (continued). This is the right-hand page. Note that the rows from the left-hand page are continued here.

Note that each passenger's last residence was now recorded, not just his or her nationality or country of origin. Since most emigrants, prior to emigrating, resided in the village or town or city of their birth, this column may provide the name of the ancestor's birthplace. At the very least, it leads the way to continued research in your ancestor's native land.

Column fourteen, "Whether in possession of money, if so, whether more than $30 and how much if $30 or less," resulted from the 1882 law requiring that arriving immigrants *not* become public charges. The minimum acceptable amount became set unofficially at $20; immigrants in possession of less than that were not admitted. Word spread among the towns and villages of Europe that $20 was sufficient to get into the United States, so rarely did arriving passengers declare more than that amount. Often they carried their entire life's savings sewn into the linings of their coats and the hems of their skirts—but they had no intention of revealing that to any official wearing a uniform!

Passenger lists were expanded, according to the 1893 law, so that the "Inspector [in the immigrant receiving center] had in his hands a written record of the immigrant he was inspecting and, asking the same questions over again, could compare the oral statements with it." The inspectors, therefore, read the names already written down on the lists and did *not*—as popular American myth persistently claims—change arbitrarily and cavalierly any immigrant's name!

The outbreak of cholera in Europe in 1893, followed by a period of economic depression in the United States that did not end until 1897, discouraged immigration during those years. From 1898, however, immigration resumed in ever-increasing numbers.

1903

In 1903, Congress added a twenty-second column to ship passenger lists to allow the federal government to keep a statistical account of the ethnic groups migrating to the shores of America:

- race or people

European empires and many smaller nations throughout the world included peoples of a variety of ethnic backgrounds. For example, an ancestor from Austria-Hungary could have been Austrian, German, Hungarian, Ukrainian, Czech, Slovak, Bohemian, Moravian, Croatian, Slovenian, Serbian, Polish, or perhaps even Italian. This new column, therefore, may help you localize your research on your immigrant ancestor's family overseas.

1906

In 1906, six more columns were added:

- personal description, including
  - height
  - complexion
  - color of hair
  - color of eyes
  - identifying marks
- place of birth

For the first time, passenger lists provided the exact city, town, or village where each passenger was born—not just his or her race or people, last residence, or nationality. This information leads you *directly* to the birthplace of your immigrant ancestor.

It was also in 1906 that the United States signed a "gentleman's agreement" with the emperor of Japan. In it, the emperor agreed that he would no longer allow his subjects to emigrate to the United States.

1907

In 1907, the information required on ship passenger lists was once again expanded, bringing the total number of columns to twenty-nine:

- name and address of closest living relative in native country

BIRTHS AND DEATHS AT SEA, STOWAWAYS, AND OTHER INFORMATION

Many Customs Passenger Lists included a separate column for recording births and deaths that occurred while the vessel was traveling to North America. On lists that did not have such a column, the information was added at the end of the list as the events occurred. The names of stowaways discovered at sea or when the vessel docked were also added to the end of the list.

To many twentieth-century Immigration Passenger Lists a second list—titled "Record of Aliens Held for Special Inquiry"—was appended after the ship had docked and the passengers had been inspected by U.S. officials. This supplemental list contains the names of all passengers who were detained for any reason. It may note, for instance, that a passenger arrived with measles and had to spend three weeks in the infirmary of the immigrant receiving station before being admitted to the United States; or it might note that a passenger was ultimately denied admittance to the United States for glaucoma or some other medical problem.

Many Immigration Passenger Lists also bear handwritten notations made by the American officials who inspected the arriving passengers. For instance, depending on the year and the laws in effect at the time, a naturalized U.S. citizen who went back to his native land and then returned with a wife and children could be required to prove his American citizenship before being allowed to reenter the country with his family. If the foreign-born citizen did not have his citizenship certificate with him, immigration officials would wire the court where the naturalization took place for the required information. The results of this inquest would be noted on the passenger's line in the list.

The U.S. officials who questioned the immigrants also made corrections on the lists. This happened when an immigrant's response varied from the information recorded on the list in the port of embarkation.

Many steamships coming to the United States in the nineteenth and twentieth centuries boarded passengers not only at the initial port of embarkation but at one or two intermediate ports as well. A ship sailing from Hamburg, Germany, for instance, might board additional passengers at Liverpool, England, and Cherbourg, France, on its way to Boston. This is why, as you search through a passenger list, you may find different ports of embarkation given on different pages of the list. This could also explain why you find your English ancestor coming to America on a German ship originally out of Hamburg. (Chapter 4 contains more about this topic under "Emigration Lists.")

There are Immigration Passenger Lists (part of Record Group 85, Records of the Immigration and Naturalization Service) for the major ports of Baltimore, Boston, New Orleans, New York, and Philadelphia; for the minor ports of Galveston, Gloucester (Mass.), New Bedford (Mass.), Portland (Maine), Providence, San Francisco, Port Townsend (Wash.), Tacoma, and Seattle; and for ports in Alabama, Florida, Georgia, and South Carolina. Once again, for fullest details, consult the *Guide to Genealogical Research at the National Archives.*

The original Customs Passenger Lists and Immigration Passenger Lists are no longer stored at the National Archives. They were all microfilmed, most in the 1940s. After the microfilming, the Customs Passenger Lists from the five major ports were given to Temple University. Today they are housed in the Temple-Balch Institute's Center for Immigration Research in Philadelphia. The original Immigration Passenger Lists were destroyed. At the National Archives, therefore, all lists are on microfilm.

Does the National Archives have a microfilm copy of the passenger list of *every* ship that arrived in *every* U.S. port between 1820 and 1954? No; the National Archives has only those lists that were turned over to it by the Customs Service and the Immigration and Naturalization Service when the U.S. government established the National Archives in 1935. Galveston lists of 1872 to 1895, for example, are nonexistent, and the lists for Charleston cover only 1820 to 1829. Some authorities say the National Archives may lack up to ten percent of the total number of passenger lists created between 1820 and 1954; others suggest that up to forty percent may be lacking. No one knows for sure. What is certain, however, is that there are thousands upon thousands of lists at the National Archives for your inspection.

Moreover, be aware that these "lists" on microfilm are not always the original passenger lists submitted upon arrival in the U.S. port. Many are copies of those originals, or perhaps abstracts of them, or transcripts prepared for the State Department. For example, the Customs Passenger Lists for Boston prior to 1883 were destroyed by fire, so State Department copies and transcripts were used in place of the missing originals of September 22, 1820, through March 31, 1874. For the period of April 1, 1874, through December 31, 1882, however, no federal arrival records have survived. Fortunately, though, arrival records created in accordance with Massachusetts *state* law serve to fill in that gap. These lists are available only at the State Archives in Boston; they are not on microfilm at the National Archives. But the passengers enumerated on them are included in the National Archives index to Boston arrivals (M625)!

The Boston "lists" illustrate that, when the microfilming and indexing were being accomplished, the most complete assemblage of arrival records for each port could be achieved only by filling in periodic gaps in the original lists with information from copies, abstracts, or transcripts—and sometimes even from non-federal records. For the purposes of the family researcher, these distinctions are rarely significant. (See Michael Tepper's *American Passenger Arrival Records* for an in-depth and thorough explanation of how the lists for each port were assembled.) What is notable is that the LDS church Family History Library has copies of virtually all of these National Archives microfilmed arrival records. This means that they may be borrowed and viewed at any LDS church family history center in the world.

The Customs Passenger Lists and Immigration Passenger Lists at the National Archives are grouped by port of arrival. Each port may include from one to more than six-thousand rolls of microfilm. Each group has a title and number, and each roll is labeled. For example, *Passenger Lists of Vessels Arriving at Boston, Mass., 1820-1891* is microfilm M277 and contains 115 rolls. Roll number one contains lists from September 22, 1820, to March 30, 1825; roll number two contains lists from April 4, 1825, to June 30, 1826; and so forth. *Passenger Lists of Vessels Arriving at Boston, Mass., 1891-1943* is microfilm T843 and comprises 454 rolls. Roll number one contains lists for 1891; roll number two contains lists for 1892; and so on. These many thousands of rolls of microfilmed passenger lists are kept in file drawers located just off the Microfilm Reading Room (room 400) at the National Archives.

NATIONAL ARCHIVES INDEXES

How do you find one passenger among the millions in all these rolls of passenger lists? Through the indexes! Fortunately for family historians, one of the undertakings of the Work Projects Administration (WPA) during the Depression was composing personal name indexes to ship passenger lists for the Immigration and Naturalization Service.

Indexers read through the lists line by line and created a three-inch by five-inch index card for each passenger (see illustration). Sufficient information was handwritten or typed onto each card to allow future researchers to identify a particular passenger and find him or her in the ship list. This information usually included the passenger's name, age, sex, occupation, country of origin, and port of departure; and the name of the ship and its date and port of arrival. The completed indexes were then microfilmed and the original cards destroyed (with rare exceptions—see Tepper's *American Passenger Arrival Records*).

These microfilmed indexes are at your disposal at the National Archives and make searching for a particular passenger a feasible undertaking. Unfortunately, the WPA workers did not complete an index for every port for every year. The indexes to passenger arrivals at the five major ports and the periods they cover are as follows:

Baltimore: 1820-1897 and 1897-1952

Boston: 1848–1891, 1902–1906, and 1906–1920

New Orleans: 1853–1899 and 1900–1952

New York: 1820–1846, 1897–1902, 1902–1943, and
1944–1948

Philadelphia: 1800–1906 and 1883–1948

Note that many of the peak years of immigration into Boston—1892 through 1901—and New York—1847 through 1896—are not indexed. Do not despair! Published indexes and other resources discussed later in this chapter exist to help you search those years.

Also note that the index to passenger arrivals at Philadelphia begins in 1800. Even before the legislation of 1819, an earlier act of Congress had exempted incoming passengers from paying duty on a limited amount of personal baggage. Authorities at the port of Philadelphia, ever scrupulous in their record-keeping, maintained lists of names of arriving passengers carrying personal baggage exceeding that limit and subject to taxation. These were called "Baggage Lists."Although the original Baggage Lists are not kept at

Family name				Given name		
ELLIS				**ROBERT**		
Accompanied by						
Age **40** Yrs.	Sex	M.	S.	Occupation	Nationality	
Mos.	**M**	W.	D.	**NOT GIVEN**	**IRELAND**	
Last permanent residence (town country, etc.)					Destination	
					U.S.	
Port of entry		N. me of vessel				Date
Philadelphia, Pa		**BARK FAIRFIELD**				**7-/7-/838**
Department of Labor, Immigration and Naturaliz on Service. Form 548-C						14—3218

Alphabetical Index Card. This sample is from National Archives microfilm M360, *Index to Passenger Lists of Vessels Arriving at Philadelphia, 1800–1906*, roll 40, "Ellis, H.–Es." It shows that Robert Ellis arrived July 17, 1858, on the bark *Fairfield*.

the National Archives (they are in the Pennsylvania State Archives in Harrisburg), they were microfilmed with the Philadelphia ship passenger lists to make the microfilm publication as complete as possible for that port. They are indexed, therefore, in the index to Philadelphia lists. Of course, the names of passengers whose personal baggage did not exceed the duty-free limit would not appear on these lists.

In addition, note that there may be some overlap of indexes to the same port. For example, the two indexes to Philadelphia arrivals overlap for the years 1883 through 1906. And a separate index to Baltimore arrivals (created originally for the city) covers the years 1833 through 1866.

There are also indexes to passenger arrivals at many minor ports:

Atlantic, Gulf Coast, and Great Lakes ports: 1820–1874

Alabama, Florida, Georgia, and South Carolina ports: 1890–1924

Detroit, Mich.: 1906–1954

Galveston, Tex.: 1896–1906 and 1906–1951

Gulfport, Miss.: 1904–1954

Pascagoula, Miss.: 1903–1935

New Bedford, Mass.: 1902–1954

Portland, Maine: 1893–1954

Providence, R.I.: 1911–1954

San Francisco, Calif.: 1893–1934

Each of these indexes has an identifying number as well as title, and each may comprise from one to more than seven-hundred rolls of microfilm. In addition, each roll is labeled: for example, *Index to Passengers Arriving at New Bedford, Mass., July 1, 1902–November 18, 1954* is microfilm T522 and comprises two rolls. Roll one is labeled "Abalo-Simas, Marie Da," and roll two is labeled "Simas, Maria Da-Zuzarte." All of these indexes are kept in file drawers near the microfilmed ship passenger lists just off room 400 at the National Archives.

Microfilm M334, *A Supplemental Index to Passenger Lists of Vessels Arriving at Atlantic and Gulf Coast Ports, 1820–1874*, must be mentioned here because its contents are often misunderstood. It covers passengers arriving at about 70 of the 101 ports in use in the nineteenth century—including minor ports such as Portland, Maine, Wilmington, Del., and Charleston, S.C., on the Atlantic; Galveston, Tex., and Mobile, Ala., on the Gulf Coast; and Rochester, N.Y., and Sandusky, Ohio, on the Great Lakes. The passenger lists of all the minor ports indexed on M334 are on microfilm M575, *Copies of Lists of Passengers Arriving at Miscellaneous Ports on the Atlantic and Gulf Coasts and at Ports on the Great Lakes, 1820–1873*. Please note, however, that M334 covers *some* passengers who arrived at all of the major ports as well—*except* New York City. (For more about this, see "M334 for Boston and New Orleans Arrivals" in Chapter 4.)

All of these indexes are one of two different kinds: those in which the passengers' surnames are listed in alphabetical order and those in which the surnames are listed according to the Soundex indexing system. Below are two sample research cases to illustrate how these indexes work.

ALPHABETICAL INDEXES

You know the three basic facts about your immigrant ancestor: his name is Ignazio Colletta; he arrived in America about 1890; and he was about thirty-six years old at the time. Knowing these facts, you are ready to begin your search. The first thing you must do, by process of elimination, is learn his port of arrival.

To do this, you search for Ignazio Colletta in every index available at the National Archives. You search Baltimore, Boston, and Philadelphia without success. The last index to turn to is the one for New Orleans since New York arrivals are not indexed for 1890. If you do not find Ignazio Colletta in the New Orleans index, you will assume he arrived at the port of New York and continue your search for his ship using the other resources and strategies discussed in Chapter 4.

The index to passenger arrivals at New Orleans is in two parts: *Index to Passenger Lists of Vessels Arriving at New Orleans, La., 1853–1899* is an alphabetical index, microfilm T527 (thirty-two rolls); *Index to Passenger Lists of Vessels Arriving at New Orleans, La., 1900–1952* is also an alphabetical index, microfilm T618 (twenty-two rolls). Since you know Ignazio Colletta arrived about 1890, you are going to use microfilm T527.

Roll number six is labeled "Claude, Joseph–Dallu, L." You take it from the file drawer and crank it through the microfilm reader until you come to a card bearing the surname Coleta. A quick glance confirms that there is a string of cards for passengers named Coleta, Coletta, Colleta, and Colletta. Familiar now with how the lists were created, you realize that any spelling could be your ancestor. You find only one Ignazio—an "Ignazio Coletta." You have completed step one of the research process!

The index card contains a number of boxes in which the indexer has transcribed from the original passenger list certain facts about the passenger. He is a thirty-six-year-old male laborer from Italy and appears in the list of the S.S. *Trinacria*, which sailed from Palermo, Sicily, and arrived in New Orleans on June 9, 1890. Could he be your ancestor? You must examine the list to know for sure, so you proceed to step two of the research process: use the information given on the index card to locate Ignazio Coletta in the list of the S.S. *Trinacria*.

You return roll number six of microfilm T527 to its drawer. (Be sure to replace the microfilm exactly where you found it!) Then you take a few steps to the file drawers containing *Passenger Lists of Vessels Arriving at New Orleans, La., 1820–1902*, microfilm M259 (ninety-three rolls). Roll number seventy-three is labeled "Oct. 2, 1889–June 25, 1890." You take it and crank it through the reader until you come to the list of the S.S. *Trinacria*. Now you search the passenger list line by line until you find "Ignazio Coletta." There he is!

His first name, age, and year of arrival all fit your ancestor perfectly, but his surname appears with only one *l*. You want to pick up on an additional fact or two in the passenger list to confirm that this man is indeed your ancestor. This you do based on prior research. First, Ignazio Coletta sailed from Palermo, Sicily, and you know your ancestor was Sicilian; Palermo would be the port closest to his native village. Second, you recognize the surnames of the four young men enumerated in the list just before Ignazio, and the five young men enumerated just after him, as those of families of your ancestor's village. Obviously, they were ten *paesani* traveling together.

Using an alphabetical index to ship passenger lists, therefore, is not difficult. Be alert to spot any evidence in the list to confirm that the passenger you have found is indeed your ancestor. But not all indexes to passenger arrivals are alphabetical; some use the Soundex system.

S.S. *Trinacria*
Courtesy of Peabody Museum of Salem

SOUNDEX INDEXES

The Soundex system was developed for the National Archives by Remington Rand Corporation in the 1930s as a means of creating personal name indexes to records according to the sounds of the names rather than their spellings. The initial letter of each name is retained, the following consonants are assigned numbers, and the vowels are ignored. The name *Schmitt*, for example, appears under the Soundex category of S-530, along with *Smith* and *Schumad* and *Sheeneth* and a variety of other names that all begin with the letter *S* and have the same subsequent consonant sounds.

Within each Soundex code, the names are alphabetized under the first letter of the *first* name. Under S-530, for example, *Schmitt, Johann*, would follow *Smith, Andrew*; *Sheeneth, Donald*, would fall between *Smith, Andrew*, and *Schmitt, Johann*.

Within each group of same *first* names, individuals are listed by order of age from youngest to oldest. A Donald who is twelve years of age would be listed in the index before a Donald who is forty-three.

There are special rules for coding surnames beginning with prefixes—such as *Di Giovanni*, *Van Camp*, and *De LaFayette*—as well as surnames containing consonant blends and double consonants. Use of the Soundex system is explained in every National Archives publication. See, for example, "Guide to the Soundex System" on page 163 of *Immigrant and Passenger Arrivals*.

The cards in the Soundex indexes are similar to those found in the alphabetical indexes (see illustration). They contain a number of boxes into which the WPA indexer transcribed from the list various data about the passenger, including name, age, sex, occupation, country of origin, port of embarkation, and, of course, the name of the ship and the date and port of its arrival.

Let us say you are looking for Domenico Geraci. He came to the United States around 1911 at about the age of forty-six. You do not know his port of arrival, but decide to begin your search with New York, since that port is a likely possibility for an Italian immigrant arriving about 1911, and it is indexed for that year. (For a word about determining an ancestor's most likely port of arrival, see "Determining Your Ancestor's Probable Port of Departure" in Chapter 4.) If you do not find Domenico Geraci in the New York index, you will proceed to search the indexes to other ports. The process of elimination will lead you to his port.

The index to passenger arrivals at New York is in four parts: *Index to Passenger Lists of Vessels Arriving at New York, N.Y., 1820–1846* is an alphabetical index, microfilm M261 (103 rolls); *Index to Passenger Lists of Vessels Arriving at New York, N.Y., June 16, 1897–June 30, 1902* is also an alphabetical index, microfilm T519 (115 rolls); but *Index (Soundex) to Passenger Lists of Vessels Arriving at New York, N.Y., July 1, 1902–December 31, 1943* is a Soundex index, microfilm T621 (755 rolls); and *Index (Soundex) to Passenger Lists of Vessels Arriving at the Port of New York, 1944–48* is also a Soundex index, microfilm M1417 (ninety-four rolls).

Since Domenico Geraci arrived about 1911, you are going to use microfilm T621. This means you will have to translate the name

Soundex Index Card. This card is from National Archives microfilm T621, *Index (SOUNDEX) to Passenger Lists of Vessels Arriving at New York, July 1, 1902–Dec. 31, 1943*, roll 551, "P-650 Armando–P-652 Marian M." It shows that Salvatore Piraino arrived April 20, 1908, on the S.S. *Florida*.

Geraci into the Soundex code; you come up with G-620. Roll number 244 is labeled "G-620 Caroline-G-620 Johann." You take it from the drawer and crank it through all the first names beginning with C and D until you find the following sequence of index cards:

> Gorga, Domenico (44 years old), with data . . .
>
> Grasso, Domenico (45 years old), with data . . .
>
> Greco, Domenico (46 years old), with data . . .
>
> Geraci, Domenico (46 years old), with data . . .

You have found a forty-six-year-old Domenico Geraci who arrived at the port of New York. Step one of the research process is accomplished. But is he your ancestor? You need to examine the passenger list to find out, so proceed to step two: use the information given on the index card to find Domenico Geraci in the passenger list. As the case of Ignazio Colletta just demonstrated, it is a simple matter of using the data from the index card to locate the passenger list and find your ancestor in it—with one exception.

POST-1910 NEW YORK ARRIVALS

The exception applies to passenger arrivals at the port of New York *only*, after 1910 *only*: a different index card was used. It gives much less information about the passenger, and this limited information is given in a simplified, numerical fashion. It is obvious from the appearance of Domenico Geraci's index card that he arrived after 1910. The card looks like this:

GERACI, Domenico 46m 3 13 3942

This means that Domenico Geraci is a forty-six-year-old male and that his name appears on line three of page 13 of volume 3942 of passenger lists. The information given on these post-1910 New York index cards, therefore, is: name, age, sex, line number, page number, and volume number. Note that there is no name of any ship and no date of arrival.

You write down this information and put roll number 244 of microfilm T621 back in the drawer. (Be sure you put it in the right place in the right drawer!) Then you walk the few steps to the file drawers containing *Passenger and Crew Lists of Vessels Arriving at New York, N.Y., 1897–1957*, microfilm T715 (8,892 rolls). Roll number 1782 of microfilm T715 is labeled "Volumes 3941–3942." You need volume 3942, so you take it and crank it through to volume 3942, crank to page 13, and then look down the page to line three: there is Domenico Geraci!

He appears as a passenger on board the S.S. *Martha Washington*, which sailed from Palermo, Sicily, on November 21, 1911, and entered New York on December 5, 1911. You are sure he is your ancestor because the name, age, and year of arrival all fit. Besides, column eleven of the list indicates that Domenico's "nearest relative or friend in country whence alien came" is his wife, Rosalia Marrone, and you know that your ancestor's wife was named Rosalia.

S.S. *Martha Washington*
Courtesy of Steamship Historical Society
Collection, University of Baltimore

The volume number derives from the fact that the old ship passenger lists were at one time gathered into volumes, which were then paginated *as volumes*. Do not let the pagination confuse you. Each individual passenger list had its own, original page numbers; then, after being gathered together into a volume, the entire batch of passenger lists was paginated as a volume. Consequently, every page of every passenger list after the first one in the volume has two numbers. It is the volume page number that is of interest to you, regardless of what number that page may happen to be of the individual list.

It is helpful, especially when dealing with common names, to know which volume numbers correspond to which years. Pages 55 through 121 of *Immigrant and Passenger Arrivals* show this correspondence from volume 1 (beginning June 16, 1897) through volume 18654 (November 27, 1954).

Using the Soundex indexes to ship passenger lists, therefore, is no more complicated than using the alphabetical indexes unless your ancestor arrived after 1910 at the port of New York. In that case, interpreting the information printed on the index card takes a little extra effort.

BOOK INDEXES

In addition to the alphabetical and Soundex indexes discussed above, there are also "book indexes" to passenger arrivals at five ports:

Boston: 1899–1940

New York: 1906–1942

Philadelphia: 1906–1926

Portland, Maine: 1907–1930

Providence, R.I.: 1911–1934

These indexes, too, were prepared for the Immigration and Naturalization Service, but not by the WPA; they were created by the various steamship lines. They have been microfilmed and are available for searching at the National Archives.

Book indexes are arranged chronologically. Under each year, they are grouped by steamship line. Within each line, they are chronological by the date of arrival of each ship. Finally, for each ship, the names of the passengers on board are listed in alphabetical order by initial letter of surname. For each passenger, an age and destination is indicated. Book indexes are most useful, therefore, when you know not only your ancestor's approximate date of arrival in the United States, but the most likely steamship line as well.

PROBLEMS WITH THE NATIONAL ARCHIVES INDEXES—AND SOLUTIONS

There are many reasons why you may, from time to time, be baffled by the National Archives indexes to ship passenger lists. For example, you may know for sure that your ancestor arrived at a port during a year that is indexed, yet you may *still* be unable to find your ancestor's name in the index.

For one thing, your ancestor's ship passenger list may have been destroyed or lost long before the lists were ever indexed. As noted above, from ten to forty percent of all lists created between 1820 and 1954 may be lacking from the National Archives' collection. No one can say for sure; a firm figure is impossible. What this means, however, is that if your ancestor arrived, for example, at Baltimore in 1827, but his name appeared in a list that was destroyed or lost before the lists were indexed, neither your ancestor's name nor the name of any other passenger traveling on that ship would appear in any index, even though passenger arrivals at the port of Baltimore during 1827 are supposedly indexed. The WPA workers could only include in their indexes, of course, the names that appeared in the lists supplied to them.

In addition, many of the lists in the custody of the Customs Service and the Immigration and Naturalization Service were already in a state of bad deterioration when they were indexed during the

Depression. A name that happened to be written on a crease or tear or had been covered by a water stain may not have been legible to the indexer; so the name, even though it appears in a list that was indexed, will *not* appear in the index.

Another consideration is the fact that a name may differ as it appears in the list and as it appears in the index to that list. In fact, the two versions of the name may bear little resemblance to one another. The lists were written in a variety of handwritings, and it was not always possible for the indexers to decipher the spelling of every name.

SOLUTIONS

If you know that your ancestor arrived at a port that is indexed for his or her year of arrival but you are unable to find your ancestor in that index, consider two possibilities:

1. Try to discover whether your ancestor was traveling with someone—perhaps a relative or neighbor from the native town. Find the name of the traveling companion in the index and note the name of his or her ship and its date of arrival. Then search the passenger list of that ship line by line; chances are you will find your ancestor enumerated right next to the traveling companion.

2. Try another port. A busy coastal steamer service connected American ports. Passengers arriving at one port sometimes continued on to another port by coastal steamer after completing immigration processing. If your grandmother insists that she arrived in Boston, for example, and you do not find her name in the index to Boston arrivals, consider the possibility that she actually entered New York, and *then* went to Boston by coastal steamer. In that case, her name would be in the index to passenger arrivals at the port of New York, *not* Boston.

Many portions of the microfilmed indexes at the National Archives are also illegible or almost illegible due to poor microfilming and subsequent use and deterioration. Below are a few helpful suggestions for dealing with hard-to-read index cards.

1. Try using either a microfilm reader that magnifies the image or a hand-held magnifying glass. Simply enlarging the faint handwriting sometimes makes it clearer.

2. You might also try placing a buff-colored sheet of paper on the microfilm reader's reading surface. Projecting the handwriting onto a light-colored sheet of paper rather than the harsh white reading surface brings out detail.

3. If you can make out only three or four letters of the name of the ship, copy those letters as you see them, leaving spaces for the letters you cannot decipher. Then search through listings of passenger ships for a name that fits those letters. (See the "Sailing Vessels and Steamships" section of the bibliography for books that list passenger ships.)

4. Likewise, if you can read the year of arrival but not the month and day, it is often possible to obtain the complete date from other sources. Two such sources, *Registers of Vessels Arriving at the Port of New York from Foreign Ports, 1789–1919* (microfilm M1066) and the *Morton-Allan Directory of European Passenger Steamship Arrivals*, are explained in detail below.

Working with the indexes to ship passenger lists at the National Archives calls for patience and persistence, but they are worth the effort. Even though they are far from complete for every port and year, they remain the most extensive indexes available for searching for individual names in passenger lists of the 1820-to-1954 period. However, if they turn out *not* to be helpful in your search, do not despair—you are far from defeated. There are other resources you may use to achieve success in your quest.

CHAPTER 4

SEARCHING IN UNINDEXED YEARS

If you know the exact day, month, and year in which your ancestor arrived in the United States, as well as the port of his or her arrival, you need use no index at all. Go straight to the microfilmed lists for that port, select the roll containing your ancestor's arrival date, and search for your ancestor's name in the lists of the ships arriving in that port on that date. Rarely, however, will you have such precise information when you undertake the search for an ancestor's ship! Most genealogists rely on the indexes for success in their search.

However, as noted previously, not all ports are indexed for all years. When the port and year of their ancestor's arrival are *not* indexed, many genealogists abandon the search or resort to searching through an entire year or two of passenger lists, roll by roll, line by line. This may mean searching through ten, fifteen, or more rolls of microfilm. Lucky researchers may discover that their ancestor arrived in the month of January, but the odds are against that. The months of heaviest immigration were in the spring—March, April, and May—and fall—September, October, and November. Your ancestor may even have arrived on December 31st. By the time you reach that roll of microfilm, you may be blurry-eyed from exhaustion and miss the name when it appears!

The tedious task of searching through list after list, line by line, *may* be alleviated if you eliminate from consideration the lists of ships that originated in ports your ancestor would probably not have used when he or she emigrated. Or, better yet, if you know your ancestor's port of departure you can skip all lists except those for ships that originated in that port. (For more about ports of embarkation, see "Emigration Lists" below.)

Nevertheless, even when you know the port of embarkation, searching through many rolls of lists, one at a time, can be prohibitively burdensome and should remain your methodology of last resort. There are more efficient, and perhaps ultimately more reliable, strategies for dealing with unindexed years that you should try first. To put them into practice, however, you must analyze your search.

First, evaluate the following resources—published indexes, microfilm M1066, microfilm M334, the *Morton-Allan Directory*, and emigration lists—by asking "What facts must I know about my ancestor's immigration story to use this resource?" Second, select those resources you are able to use based on the facts you know. Third, arrange those resources in descending order from the most likely to lead to success to the least promising. Finally, begin with the first!

PUBLISHED INDEXES

Chapter 2 focused on the wide variety of indexes to *published*, pre-1820 arrival records that are available in libraries. In addition to these, however, libraries hold an increasing number of indexes to *unpublished* arrival records dating from 1820—that is, indexes to ship passenger lists in the National Archives. These indexes focus on passengers of a particular nationality, on passengers arriving at a particular port, or on passengers arriving during a particular span of years. Many of them overlap the microfilmed indexes at the National Archives. (Indeed, some are simply transcripts of portions of National Archives indexes.) Others, however, complement National Archives indexes by filling in some of the gaps of unindexed years. These published indexes are the ones that may be decisively helpful to family historians searching for an ancestor in a year for which no National Archives index exists. (See the bibliography for the major indexes to unpublished arrival records.)

As long as you know your immigrant ancestor's full, original name, approximate age at arrival, and approximate date of arrival, you are prepared to use these indexes. Simply focus your search on indexes that cover the time period in which your ancestor arrived—and hope that your ancestor's name appears. However, the more you know, the more you can narrow your search.

Below are two research scenarios that demonstrate how to use published indexes to find your ancestor in a National Archives ship passenger list when you know some additional fact, such as your ancestor's nationality or port of arrival. For each suggested index, refer to the bibliography for complete publication data and annotations. As always when using any reference text, be sure to read the introduction carefully to understand precisely *what* records are indexed and *how* they are indexed. Reading book titles alone may mislead you!

IF YOU KNOW YOUR ANCESTOR'S NATIONALITY

Search for your ancestor's name in indexes to National Archives lists compiled by nationality, such as:

Glazier, Ira A., ed. *The Famine Immigrants: Lists of Irish Immigrants Arriving at the Port of New York, 1846–1851.*

Glazier, Ira A., and P. William Filby, eds. *Germans to America: Lists of Passengers Arriving at U.S. Ports.* Published to date—1850–72.

IF YOU KNOW YOUR ANCESTOR'S PORT OF ARRIVAL

Search for your ancestor's name in indexes to National Archives lists compiled by port of arrival, such as:

Rasmussen, Louis J. *San Francisco Ship Passenger Lists.* Published to date—1850–75.

Southern Historical Press. *Ship Passenger Lists, Port of Galveston, Texas, 1846–1871.*

Note that each of these indexes focuses on a specific national group, port, and span of years; they are far from comprehensive. Nevertheless, the time periods they cover complement the years covered by indexes at the National Archives, which may make such a published index the critical element to success in your quest. Some are ongoing, with a new volume appearing every year; so if your ancestor's year has not yet been indexed, you may only have to be patient and wait for the next volume!

If you find your ancestor's name in one of these indexes, step one of your search is done. Proceed to step two: use the data provided in the index to locate the passenger list in the National Archives. Place the pertinent roll of microfilm in the reader and find your ancestor's name in the list; then, double- check the information you find against your ancestor's full, original name, approximate age at arrival, and approximate date of arrival to be certain the passenger is *your* ancestor and not someone else's!

How do you search for an ancestor's ship when there is no National Archives index *and* no published index covering the port and years of interest to you? There are resources *other* than indexes at your disposal! . . .

MICROFILM M1066—FOR NEW YORK ARRIVALS

If your immigrant ancestor arrived at the port of New York during one of the years for which there is no index to passenger arrivals— 1847 through 1896—one useful resource to help you find the ship is microfilm M1066, *Registers of Vessels Arriving at the Port of New York from Foreign Ports, 1789-1919* (twenty-seven rolls). This microfilm publication is the most complete list available of the ships that entered New York from foreign ports between 1789 and 1919.

Any single publication comprised of so many volumes of records and created by a variety of offices for a variety of purposes, over a time period exceeding a century, will inevitably contain many inconsistencies. These volumes vary a great deal in their internal arrangement, as well as in the amount and type of information they record. Most of the volumes contain at least the following for each vessel listed: name, country of origin, type of rig, date of entry, master's name, and last port of embarkation (see illustration). Some volumes contain additional information as well: in some years, the

Page from a Register of Vessels. This sample is from National Archives microfilm M1066, *Registers of Vessels Arriving at the Port of New York from Foreign Ports, 1789–1919*, roll 8, "Jan. 2–Dec. 31, 1856." It shows that the bark *Elbe*, Captain Winzen, arrived May 21, 1856, from Hamburg, Germany.

ships are listed in their chronological order of arrival; in other years, the ships are listed in alphabetical order, regardless of their exact date of arrival; in still other years, the ships are grouped by steamship line.

Regardless of how the information may be arranged, however, microfilm M1066 may be helpful in your search if you know: 1) the name of your ancestor's ship; 2) its exact date of arrival; or 3) your ancestor's port of departure. To demonstrate, let us say that your ancestor, Andreas Schlager, came from Bavaria in 1886 with his wife, Ursula.

IF YOU KNOW THE NAME OF THE SHIP

Select the roll of M1066 that corresponds to the year of your ancestor's arrival, and make note of every date on which his or her ship entered New York that year. Then turn to the New York passenger lists, microfilm M237, and search the lists of your ancestor's ship, one by one, line by line, for the arrival dates you noted. Your ancestor's name should appear in one of them.

You know from oral family tradition that Andreas Schlager came on the S.S. *Werra*. Using M1066, you learn that the S.S. *Werra* entered New York harbor eight times in 1886: March 6th, April 5th, May 1st, May 28th, July 8th, August 23rd, October 7th, and November 17th. Taking the New York passenger lists, microfilm M237, you search the lists of the S.S. *Werra* for those eight arrival dates. You find an Andreas Schlager in the list for the crossing that terminated on May 28, 1886. Enumerated with him is his wife, Ursula—proof that you have found *your* Andreas Schlager and not someone else's.

When dealing with sailing vessels in earlier years, you will probably not collect more than three to five dates, since rigged vessels made fewer crossings each year than the later, faster steamships. (See "Sailing Vessels and Steamships" below.)

This same strategy may be used in reverse: use it when you do *not* know the name of the ship but you *do* know the exact date of arrival.

If You Know the Exact Date of Arrival

You know from Andreas Schlager's naturalization record that he arrived at the port of New York on May 28, 1886, but you do not know in what ship. Select the roll of M1066 that contains the date May 28, 1886, and make note of every ship that entered New York harbor that day; it turns out to be twelve ships in all.

Eliminate all the unlikely candidates: three ships arrived from South American ports (Rio de Janeiro, Brazil; Cartagena, Chile; and Montevideo, Uruguay); three ships came from the Caribbean (Havanna and Cienfuegos, Cuba; and Kingston, Jamaica); two from the Orient (Yokohama, Japan; and Hong Kong); one from Marseilles, France; and one from Liverpool, England. Eliminating those ships leaves two possibilities: the S.S. *Moravia* out of Hamburg and the S.S. *Werra* out of Bremen.

Turn then to the New York passenger lists, microfilm M237, and search the lists of those two liners. You discover Andreas and Ursula Schlager on the list of the S.S. *Werra*.

Even if you do not know the name of the ship *or* its exact date of arrival, microfilm M1066 may be useful if you know from which port your ancestor emigrated.

If You Know the Port of Embarkation

Since Andreas Schlager was Bavarian by birth, it is most likely that he emigrated from the port of Bremen. (For tips on determining an ancestor's probable port of departure, see "Emigration Lists" below.) Using microfilm M1066, select from all of the passenger ships arriving in New York in 1886 only those that originated in Bremen. Search the lists of these ships for your forefather; you will find him on the S.S. *Werra*.

Be advised, however, that this strategy may still leave you with an unmanageable number of lists to search if your ancestor left from a *busy* port in the *late* nineteenth century—as did Andreas Schlager. By 1886, ships from Bremen were entering New York harbor about ninety-five times each year. It is possible, of course, that your ancestor came on one of the early voyages; in this case, you will not have to search through all ninety-five lists. He may have come around the middle of the year—May 28th—like Andreas Schlager. But then, he may have come on the last voyage of the year. . . .

Microfilm M1066 may be a valuable resource, therefore, because searching through two or three, even fifteen or twenty—perhaps even ninety-five!—passenger lists is far preferable to searching through thirteen or fourteen entire rolls of microfilm. A portion of microfilm M1066 has recently been published in book form under the title *Passenger Ships Arriving in New York Harbor (1820–1850)*, edited by Bradley W. Steuart. Future volumes covering additional years are planned.

The National Archives has journals of, and alphabetical indexes to, vessel arrivals at ports *other* than New York as well; these include Boston, Philadelphia, Baltimore, and New Orleans. They are part of Record Group 36, Records of the U.S. Customs Service. But these have not been organized and microfilmed as New York's have, so they are less accessible, though not impossible to exploit in a manner similar to M1066.

SAILING VESSELS AND STEAMSHIPS

As the example of Andreas Schlager shows, it may prove helpful to your search to know whether your ancestor arrived in a sailing vessel or a steamship. Steamships began making regular crossings of the Atlantic in the 1850s. Steamship companies advertised that they could maintain a regular schedule, regardless of wind and current; and steamships crossed the ocean in less than half the time it took sailing vessels. But the transatlantic fares of sailing ships remained for many years much cheaper than those of steamships, so many immigrants, most of whom were poor, continued into the 1870s to endure the discomfort and uncertainty of reaching the United States under sail. By the 1880s, however, steam had effectively replaced sail forever.

Sailing vessels might take anywhere from four to twelve weeks to cross the Atlantic; they might take longer if they encountered adverse winds or currents. A normal, uneventful transatlantic voyage by sail lasted eight weeks. Steamships crossed in two to three weeks during the nineteenth century and up to World War I, depending on the number of intermediate ports the vessel visited on its way to the United States. That travel time was shortened to one to two weeks by the 1920s, and by World War II steamships from Europe could reach America in just five days.

THE MORTON-ALLAN DIRECTORY—FOR NEW YORK, BALTIMORE, BOSTON, AND PHILADELPHIA ARRIVALS

Another resource for finding ships that arrived during unindexed years is the *Morton-Allan Directory of European Passenger Steamship Arrivals*. This volume is similar to microfilm M1066 and the unmicrofilmed registers of vessel entrances at other ports, and it can be used in a similar fashion. It lists by year, and thereunder by steamship line, the names and dates of arrival of all passenger liners that came from Europe to New York from 1890 to 1930 and to Baltimore, Boston, and Philadelphia from 1904 to 1926. If you know your ancestor arrived at one of these ports in one of these years, implement any one of the three strategies demonstrated below:

IF YOU KNOW THE NAME OF THE SHIP

Note every date on which that ship arrived during the year in which your ancestor came to America, then search through those lists.

IF YOU KNOW THE EXACT DATE OF ARRIVAL

Note the names of all ships that arrived on that date. Eliminate the unlikely ones, then search through the lists of the remaining ships.

IF YOU KNOW THE MOST PROBABLE STEAMSHIP LINE

Select, from all of the ships arriving during the year in which your ancestor entered the United States, only those of the most probable steamship line, then search the lists of the ships of that line. (If you are concerned with a time period toward the end of the nineteenth century, this strategy may still not reduce the number of lists to a number practical for searching.)

The Morton-Allan Directory—as well as other vessel arrival records—may prove useful in other ways as well, depending on your research scenario and how creative a researcher you are. For example, you may use it to verify or correct arrival information.

I was once searching for an immigrant who came in 1928. I knew the name of the ship, but I was told that the port of entry was New York, and my research showed that no ship by that name arrived in New York at that time. Finding the ship in the Morton-Allan Directory, I discovered that it regularly entered the port of Boston—not New York—and I noted the precise dates in 1928 when it arrived. Then I turned to the microfilmed passenger lists for Boston (microfilm T843), searched the lists for those arrival dates, and found the name of the immigrant I sought.

MICROFILM M334—FOR BOSTON AND
NEW ORLEANS ARRIVALS

As stated in Chapter 3, the Index to Passenger Lists of Vessels Arriving at Boston begins with the year 1848, and the Index to Passenger Lists of Vessels Arriving at New Orleans begins in 1853. However, some Boston arrivals between 1820 and 1847 and some New Orleans arrivals between 1820 and 1850 are included in microfilm M334, A Supplemental Index to Passenger Lists of Vessels Arriving at Atlantic and Gulf Coast Ports, 1820–1874, already referred to in Chapter 2. Microfilm M334 also includes some Philadelphia and Baltimore arrivals. In fact, the only port lacking entirely from the index is New York.

Therefore, if your ancestor came to any port, minor or major (other than New York), between 1820 and 1874, your search of National Archives indexes is not exhaustive until you have examined M334. It is a common misconception that M334 indexes only the sixty-seven minor ports for which lists are included on microfilm

M575; however, M334 includes at least some arrivals at four of the five major ports as well.

EMIGRATION LISTS

Ship passenger lists are sometimes called "arrival lists" or "arrival records" because they enumerate passengers *arriving* in the United States from foreign ports. However, ports of embarkation overseas also kept lists of passengers *departing* for foreign destinations, including the United States. Such "emigration lists" may prove valuable to researchers looking for an ancestor's ship in an unindexed year.

DETERMINING YOUR ANCESTOR'S PROBABLE PORT OF DEPARTURE

To determine through which port your ancestor may have emigrated to North America, you must know where he or she resided prior to departure. A reliable history of your ancestor's homeland will tell you when emigration movements occurred and what route the emigrants followed.

For example, during the 1700s and into the 1820s, emigrants from along the Rhine River—from Switzerland, Baden, Württemberg, Alsace, or Lorraine, for instance—generally took a boat down the Rhine to Rotterdam or Antwerp and sailed to North America from there. Traveling by water was the cheapest (albeit the slowest) way to get to a port city. By the 1840s, however, railroads in France and Germany had made traveling overland to Le Havre—the French port on the English Channel—more attractive than the earlier river route. A faster journey meant less money expended on food and lodging. From that time, therefore, Le Havre replaced Rotterdam and Antwerp as the most probable port of departure for emigrants from the Central European region along the Rhine.

Karl Wittke's *We Who Built America: The Saga of the American Immigrant* (see bibliography) discusses the emigration routes of a variety of national groups from Europe. A history devoted solely to your own ancestor's national group, however, is more likely to provide the detailed information you seek.

These same types of works, and the ever-flourishing ethnic histories referred to in Chapter 1, frequently provide information about which ports emigrants used to *enter* North America. Knowing your ancestor's probable port of entry may also prove useful to your search, as noted in the Domenico Geraci example in Chapter 3.

LOCATING EMIGRATION LISTS

Once you know your ancestor's most probable port of departure, how do you learn whether any emigration lists exist for that port? Begin by looking at Chapter 15 of *The Source: A Guidebook of American Genealogy* (see bibliography). It includes a table of many European ports that shows what emigration records still exist for each port, whether they are published, whether they are indexed, and how to access them. For ports not covered in this table, examine a guide to genealogical research for the country whose port interests you.

BREMEN PASSENGER LISTS

From the mid-nineteenth century through the early twentieth century, the busiest European port of embarkation was Bremen, Germany. Millions of emigrants from northern, central, and eastern Europe left from Bremen, and the port maintained lists of departing passengers. Unfortunately, all of those lists have been destroyed. Nevertheless, three resources that "reproduce" portions of the lost Bremen Passenger Lists could be of value to Americans searching for their ancestors' ships:

1. The Deutsches Ausland-Institut in Stuttgart created a card file titled "Namenskartei aus den 'Bremer Schiffslisten,' 1904–1914," which is now housed in the German State Archives in Koblenz. The LDS church Family History Library has a copy of this card file on ten reels of microfilm. The cards contain the names of emigrants based on the Bremen Passenger Lists. The first two reels contain cards arranged alphabetically by state—Anhalt-Posen through Würt-

temberg—then by surname (not necessarily in alphabetical order). The other eight reels contain cards arranged by country—Austria, Bohemia, Moravia, Hungary, Russia, Jewish Emigrants, and "Other Lands"—then by surname (not necessarily in alphabetical order).

Note that these cards do not constitute a comprehensive list of emigrants leaving from Bremen. The first two reels name only German emigrants. The other eight reels contain emigrants of other nationalities for sporadic dates of departure. Nevertheless, this card file contains thousands of emigrants' names and should not be overlooked.

2. Transcripts of a few Bremen Passenger Lists are also housed in the German State Archives in Koblenz. They cover March 1907 through November 1908 and portions of the years 1913 and 1914. (Reportedly, these transcripts are included on reels 403 and 404 of the "Captured German Documents" on microfilm at the National Archives.)

3. Gary J. Zimmerman and Marion Wolfert have published what might be called a "partial reconstruction" of the Bremen Passenger Lists (see bibliography). Using ship passenger lists at the National Archives, they have extracted the names of German passengers aboard vessels that sailed from Bremen to New York and listed those names in alphabetical order in four volumes. The volumes cover the years 1847 through 1871. Note, however, that only German passengers for whom a specific place of origin was noted in the lists are included in Zimmerman and Wolfert's index—about twenty-one percent of the total number of German passengers leaving the port of Bremen.

HAMBURG PASSENGER LISTS

The second-busiest port of embarkation from Europe was Hamburg. Happily, the original passenger lists for the port of Hamburg covering the years 1850 through 1934 are still preserved in the German State Archives in Hamburg, and they are indexed. These emigration records—probably the most informative and extensive of any European port—are particularly useful to Americans searching for ancestors' ships, since millions of Americans are descended from northern, central, and eastern Europeans who left their homelands between 1850 and 1934 via Hamburg.

The lists and the indexes to them are gathered into 517 volumes. A microfilm copy of these volumes is retained in the Historic Emigration Office at the Museum for Hamburg History. (The Historic Emigration Office is established in what used to be the officers' mess of the S.S. *Werner*.) A copy of this microfilm is available through the LDS church Family History Library. The Library of Congress in Washington, D.C., has a copy of the microfilm for the years 1850 through 1873 only.

The Hamburg lists contain not only the name of each departing passenger's ship, its date of departure, and its port of destination but also each passenger's age, birthplace, and occupation. Therefore, if you find your ancestor in the Hamburg lists, all you need to do to find the ship passenger list in the National Archives is add a sufficient amount of time to the embarkation date for the vessel to cross the Atlantic—considering whether it was a sailing vessel or a steamship—and search the ship passenger lists of the port of arrival for that time period.

Though the Hamburg lists and the indexes to them are written in German handwriting, and though they contain the peculiarities described below, they are not prohibitively difficult to use. (For a detailed explanation of the lists and their indexes, see the article by Laraine K. Ferguson or the work published by the Genealogical Department of the LDS church, both cited in the bibliography.) However, searching the Hamburg lists for an ancestor's name requires that you bear in mind two crucial factors:

1. The lists are divided into two categories: *Listen Direkt* (Direct Lists) and *Listen Indirekt* (Indirect Lists). Direct Lists enumerate passengers boarding ships that sailed directly to their destinations without stopping at other ports. Indirect Lists enumerate passengers boarding ships that stopped at intermediate European or British ports on the way to their final destinations.

2. Prior to 1911, the Direct and Indirect Lists were bound and indexed separately. The Direct Lists of 1850 through 1854 have no index because none is needed: the passengers are enumerated in alphabetical order (by first letter of surname) for each of these years. For the period 1855 through 1910, each year has an alphabetical index (by first letter of surname) for every ship, and the ships are indexed one after the other in the chronological order of their departure from Hamburg. One index volume covers the lists of 1855 and 1856, another covers the lists of 1857 and 1858, another covers 1859 through 1861, and so on.

For the Indirect Lists, 1855 through 1910, there is a single alphabetical index (by first letter of surname) for each year that covers all the ships that left that year. The index to the Indirect Lists comprises several volumes. Beginning with 1911 the two categories of lists—Direct and Indirect—were bound together and indexed together.

Let us say you are searching for your ancestor, Heim Schwien. He was about fifty-four years old when he brought his family over from their native Germany around the year 1856. You suspect that he sailed from the port of Hamburg.

First, you find the volume of the index to the Direct Lists that includes 1856—that happens to be volume 8. You search through all the surnames beginning with S for the first "direct ship" that left Hamburg that year, then the second ship, then the third, and so forth. You come to "12/4 Elbe, Winzen n/New York" (12 April, ship Elbe, Captain Winzen, to New York), and find a Heim Schwien listed "m/frau u. kind" (with wife and children); the page reference is "79" (see illustration). This could be your ancestor.

You take the Direct Lists for 1856—they happen to comprise volume 10—and turn to page 79. There is the list of passengers boarding the ship *Elbe* under Captain Winzen, departing Hamburg on April 12, 1856, and destined for New York (see illustration). Heim Schwien, a fifty-four-year-old bridle maker from Heringsdorf, is listed with his wife, Maria, and four children. It is clear from all this data that you have the right family.

Direct List Index. This sample page is from LDS church Family History Library microfilm 473,070, *Index [Direct, Vol. 8]*, 1855–1856. It shows that Heim Schwien, listed under "12/4 Elbe, Winzen n/New York," can be found (with his wife and children) on page 79 of the direct list.

Direct List for 1856, Page 79. This is from LDS church Family History Library microfilm 470,838, *Passenger Lists [Direct, Vol. 10, Part I], 1856.* It shows Heim Schwien and family on lines 17 through 22.

Estimating that it took a minimum of four weeks for the *Elbe* to cross the Atlantic, you begin your search of the passenger lists for the port of New York (microfilm M237) around mid-May. (Or, in this instance, since you are dealing with the port of New York, you might use M1066 to pinpoint the arrival date of the *Elbe* and *then* turn to the lists on M237.) You come to the list of the bark *Elbe* and learn that it arrived on May 21, 1856 (see illustration). The Schwien family is there—your search is over.

If you had *not* found your ancestor in the index to the Direct Lists, you would have proceeded to take the volume of the index to the Indirect Lists that covers 1856—which happens to be volume 1—and search through all of the surnames beginning with S for all of the "indirect ships" that left Hamburg in 1856.

Conducting a thorough search of the Hamburg lists, therefore, requires logic and concentration and some familiarity with a few key German terms. But a small amount of practice leads to increased ease and competence in using this valuable resource, and it may pay off in a big way—with the ship of your immigrant ancestor!

If, however, you prefer to have the Hamburg lists searched for you, write to the Historic Emigration Office, where staff members perform limited searches for a fee: Historic Emigration Office, c/o Tourist Information am Hafen, Bei den St.-Pauli-Landungsbrücken 3, P.O. Box 102249, D-2000 Hamburg 1, Germany.

EUROPEAN PASSPORT RECORDS

A resource closely related to emigration lists that may be used in a similar fashion for finding your ancestor's ship are European passport records. Many European countries have maintained records of passport applications submitted by prospective emigrants and of passports granted to them. A manual about genealogical research in your ancestor's native country will address this topic. If you can discover a passport record for your ancestor, it will give you an idea of when he or she may have left the country.

How much time should you allow between the granting of a passport and departure? That will vary widely from one period to

Ship Passenger List. This is from National Archives microfilm M237, *Passenger Lists of Vessels Arriving at New York, 1820–1897*, roll 162, May 15–June 9, 1856. Again, note Heim Schwien and family listed on lines 17 through 22.

another and from one locality to another. Consult those scholarly works about the emigration pattern of your ancestor's national or ethnic or religious group referred to in "Determining Your Ancestor's Probable Port of Departure" above.

Add to the approximate departure date the amount of time it would take to cross the Atlantic in that era (by sail and/or steam); this gives you an estimated arrival date. Then search for your ancestor's name in the ship passenger lists at the National Archives for that estimated arrival date.

This strategy was necessary to find my ancestor, Nicholas Miller, on the ship *Nile* (referred to in the Introduction) because the list of that ship, for unknown reasons, escaped the WPA indexers. Its passengers do not appear in the *Index to Passenger Lists of Vessels Arriving at New York, NY, 1820–1846* (microfilm M261). However, I learned that Nicholas Miller had been granted an overseas passport in Metz, Lorraine, on February 17, 1830. Based on scholarly studies of Lorrainian emigration in that era, I allowed about four weeks for the emigrant to sell his belongings and reach Le Havre. Then, confident that Nicholas Miller would have traveled by sail, not steam, I added another eight weeks for him to cross the ocean. My search of the passenger lists of ships entering the port of New York began with those of mid-May 1830, and I found that the *Nile* had arrived on the 24th—with the entire extended Miller family in steerage.

Using European passport records is neither as convenient nor as precise as using emigration lists. (Had I known that the winter of 1829–1830 was unusually severe and that the large Miller party had to wait a full week in Le Havre for the ice in the port to break up, my estimated arrival time would have been closer to the truth.) However, passport records are worth the effort when other strategies have not led to success.

If you do not know enough facts about your ancestor's immigration story to use *any* of the resources discussed above, seek more of the records described in "Where Can You Find This Information?" in the Introduction. Continue to gather specific facts until you have enough to pursue one of the strategies suggested here or to develop one of your own.

OTHER RESOURCES AND INFORMATION
OF POTENTIAL VALUE

CREW LISTS

Many American families treasure the oral tradition that their immigrant ancestor "worked his way to America" as a member of the crew on a ship bound for the United States; or that the immigrant ancestor was a crew member who "jumped ship" when the vessel entered port. (The expression "jumped ship" means that the crew member entered the United States without legal documentation, *not* that he literally leapt from the vessel into the water!) For these families, the crew lists on microfilm at the National Archives may help prove or disprove the tradition.

There are crew lists for vessels arriving at:

Boston: 1917–1943

Detroit: 1946–1957

Gloucester, Mass.: 1918–1943

New Bedford, Mass.: 1917–1943

New Orleans: 1910–1945

New York: 1897–1957

San Francisco: 1896–1954

Seattle: 1890–1957

These lists may include the names of both American and alien seamen, but the amount of information provided about each crew member varies. The information may include his length of service at sea, position in the ship's company, when and where he joined the vessel's crew, and whether he was to be discharged at the port of arrival; and his age, race, nationality, height, weight, and literacy.

LISTS OF CHINESE PASSENGERS

By the terms of the Chinese Exclusion Act of 1882 (see Chapter 3), the U.S. government began keeping special enumerations of Chinese entering the country at the major West Coast ports. Today these enumerations are useful to Chinese Americans searching for their ancestors' ships. The National Archives has on microfilm lists of Chinese passengers arriving at San Francisco in the period 1882 through 1914; lists of Chinese applying for admission to the United States through the port of San Francisco, 1903 through 1947; and lists of Chinese passengers arriving at the ports of Seattle and Port Townsend, 1882 through 1916.

NEWSPAPER OF THE PORT OF ENTRY

Sometimes the ship passenger list at the National Archives lacks the date of departure from the foreign port. You may want this information to know how long your ancestors' journey to America lasted and precisely when they left their homeland. A ship's date of departure may be secured from the newspaper of the port where the ship arrived.

Locate a repository that has newspapers for the port where your ancestor entered the United States. Read through the issues for the day the ship arrived and the following day. Newspapers of port cities always reported arriving vessels and often printed information about them and the passengers who disembarked. The names of all cabin passengers were frequently printed; steerage passengers were accounted for in a global figure.

For example, the *Nile* (referred to above) sailed into New York harbor on May 24, 1830, but the passenger list does not give the date on which the vessel left Le Havre. The *New York American* of Monday evening, May 24, 1830, indicates on page 2 that "the Ship Nile, John Rockett, Captain, arrived from Havre, sailed evening of the 4th of April." The notice goes on to state that the *Nile* brought merchandise for Jones & Megrath, names nine cabin passengers, and concludes that there were "120 in steerage." (The *New York Daily Advertiser* carried the same notice that day.) It was from the newspaper item, therefore, that I learned that it took my ancestors seven weeks and two days to cross the Atlantic. (Which, in turn, allowed me to investigate weather conditions in Le Havre in late March and early May 1830.)

The sample case explained in Chapter 2 showed that Ignazio Colletta arrived in New Orleans from Palermo on the S.S. *Trinacria* on June 9, 1890. That list, too, lacked the date of departure. But an item in *The Daily Picayune–New Orleans* titled "Immigrants from Italy" that appeared on Tuesday, June 10, 1890, provides not only the date of departure—May 14, 1890—but detailed information about the size and ownership of the S.S. *Trinacria*. The item also included the ship's entire itinerary (it had called at three intermediate ports) and an account of weather conditions at each of those points along the route.

Newspapers will report anything unusual about the arrival of your ancestor's ship—whether it was detained in quarantine because contagious disease had broken out on board, for example. Such information complements the facts you find in the list, filling in your ancestor's immigration story.

IMMIGRATION VIA CANADA, 1895–1954

During most of the nineteenth century the United States government kept no record of immigrants arriving by land from Canada. The first immigration inspection stations along the Canadian border were established by a congressional act of 1891 because by that time about forty percent of the passengers arriving in Canada were bound for the United States.

In 1895, the United States and Canada established a joint inspection system. Passengers arriving in Canada but bound for the United States were enumerated on U.S. immigration lists and inspected by U.S. officials in the Canadian port of entry. These immigrants were issued inspection cards that they surrendered to U.S. officials on board the trains as they crossed the border.

Two sets of records, therefore, were created regarding these immigrants: passenger lists and compiled inspection cards. These records were microfilmed by the Immigration and Naturalization Service in the 1950s and are available for inspection at the National Archives in the form of five microfilm publications. Together they cover Canadian border entries from 1895 through 1954 and are almost entirely indexed by individual passenger name. (For complete information about these microfilm publications, see the article by Constance Potter listed in the bibliography.)

IMMIGRATION LAWS OF 1921 AND 1924

The Emergency Quota Act was passed by the U.S. Congress and signed by President Harding on May 19, 1921. It established, for the first time in American history, not just stricter regulations for admitting aliens into the United States—that kind of law had been passed earlier, as noted in Chapters 2 and 3 above—but *numerical quotas* for immigration. This was what many European and Japanese families had feared: families were split by an ocean and had no idea when, if ever, they would be reunited.

The Emergency Quota Act was called "emergency" legislation because it had been instigated by panicked American workers who were worried about the ever-rising tide of poor, uneducated European and Japanese laborers flooding the United States work force. The American workers maintained that the immigrants undercut their salaries or deprived them of their livelihoods altogether. The "National Origins Formula" of this law was calculated to be strictest against southern and eastern Europeans and the Japanese, who constituted the majority of immigrants in the years just prior to World War I.

The Emergency Quota Act was intended as a temporary measure—expiring on June 30, 1922—to allow Congress sufficient time to debate the immigration issue and legislate a definitive resolution to the problem. But the issue was controversial and perplexing, the debate personal and emotional. Congress needed more time, so the law was extended for two additional years, to expire on June 30, 1924.

Many Europeans, though, could not wait. Rumors spread through the towns and villages of southern and eastern Europe that America would admit no more immigrants; or that men could immigrate but not women; or that men already in America could stay but could never be joined by their spouses and children. . . .

Many desperate Europeans were ready to take desperate action. Southern and eastern Europeans flocked to northern European ports to book passage on northern European vessels; somehow, this stratagem worked. You may discover that a southern or eastern European ancestor who came to the United States between 1921 and 1924 left Europe from Liverpool, Le Havre, or Bremen.

Congress finally legislated a complex set of rules to allow for the unification of separated alien families in certain cases and under certain circumstances. This legislation was contained in the Immigration Act signed into law by President Coolidge on May 21, 1924. Visas—another first in American history—became a requirement for entry into the United States. By requiring that emigrants be approved for admission into the United States before leaving their native lands, Congress put an end to the practice—common before 1924—of turning away unacceptable immigrants at the American port of arrival and sending them home. Thousands of Europeans and Japanese got their numbers and began to wait their turns. This new legislation, however, was of little concern to the many Europeans who had managed to make it into the United States through the "back door" of northern Europe.

OBTAINING A PICTURE OF YOUR ANCESTOR'S SHIP

SAILING VESSELS AND STEAMSHIPS

Three museums devoted to the history of seafaring and ships may supply more information about, and possibly pictures of, your ancestor's sailing vessel or steamship: Mystic Seaport Museum, 50 Greenmanville Avenue, Mystic, Conn. 06355; Peabody Museum, East India Square, Salem, Mass. 01970; Mariners Museum, 100 Museum Drive, Newport News, Va. 23606.

Mystic Seaport Museum has the most extensive collection of materials relating to sailing ships; Peabody Museum and Mariners Museum hold more materials relating to steamships. Moreover, the vast majority of sailing ship materials in all three museums pertains to nineteenth-century vessels. For earlier periods, you must rely on books about ships in your local public library.

THE STEAMSHIP HISTORICAL SOCIETY OF AMERICA

The Steamship Historical Society of America is a national organization of individuals interested in the history of steamships, both freight and passenger, from the earliest ones of the 1830s through those of the twentieth century. Its extensive collection of books, manuscripts, and steamship memorabilia is conserved in the Steamship Historical Society of America Collection, Ann House, Librarian, Langsdale Library, University of Baltimore, 1420 Maryland Avenue, Baltimore, Md. 21201; (410) 837-4334

The collection does not include any original passenger lists, but it does include about 100,000 engravings, drawings, and photographs of steamships. Once you know the name of the ship that brought your ancestor to the United States, you can have the collection searched for a picture of it. If there is one in the collection, the society will have a copy of that picture made for you for a nominal fee.

The society can also provide technical information about particular steamships, such as registry, tonnage, year of construction, and so forth. You may learn much about your ancestor's ship even if you cannot find a picture of it. In addition, the bibliography at the end of this volume lists several works that provide information and photographs of the steamships that carried our ancestors to America.

A WORD ABOUT ELLIS ISLAND

It is estimated that while Ellis Island was operating as an immigrant receiving station—1892 through 1924—17 million men, women, and children passed through its doors. That may be true, but the figure is misleading. It is presumably based on the total number of names appearing on the ship passenger lists for the port of New York during those years. But a substantial number of the passengers named on those lists came two, three, or more times, and many others did not remain in the United States permanently. Taking these facts into account, statisticians estimate that roughly 12 million immigrants who became permanent residents of the United States passed through Ellis Island.

The figure is nonetheless impressive, and it justifies Ellis Island's preeminent status in the history of U.S. immigration. However, many Americans, thoroughly familiar with that red brick and limestone icon, forget that not *every* immigrant coming to America passed through Ellis Island!

In colonial times, as noted in Chapter 1, numerous ports were used by immigrant settlers, and there were no receiving stations at all to process them. Even in the nineteenth and twentieth centuries, as Chapter 3 has shown, immigrants to the United States arrived at many minor ports—including the oft-forgotten Pacific Coast ports of San Francisco, Seattle and Port Townsend—in addition to the major ports of Boston, New York, Philadelphia, Baltimore, and New Orleans. What is more, not all immigrants who arrived at New York passed through Ellis Island! Consider this chronology of the immigrant receiving center for the port of New York:

August 1, 1855–April 18, 1890: Castle Garden
April 19, 1890–December 31, 1891: Barge Office
January 1, 1892–June 13, 1897: Ellis Island
June 14, 1897–December 16, 1900: Barge Office
December 17, 1900–1924: Ellis Island

The state of New York founded this country's first center for examining and processing arriving immigrants in 1855. It was established in Castle Garden on an island off the southwest tip of Manhattan. (The circular, red stone foundation of Castle Garden stands today in Battery Park.) One purpose of the center was to help U.S. health officials prevent people with contagious diseases from entering the country. But it was also hoped that a receiving station located off the mainland would serve to relieve the horrors—fraud, robbery, deceit, kidnapping—that afflicted immigrants the moment they stepped onto land.

On April 18, 1890, when the Secretary of the Treasury terminated the contract his department held with the New York State Commissioners of Emigration—see Chapter 3—and assumed total control of immigration affairs at the harbor, New York state officials were not pleased. They refused to allow the federal government the use of Castle Garden, and Castle Garden's career as an immigrant receiving station ended.

The following day, therefore—April 19, 1890—the U.S. government established a temporary processing center in the old Barge Office at the southeast foot of Manhattan (near the U.S. Customs House). About 525,000 immigrants would be processed through the old Barge Office during the one year and eight months it served this purpose. A small, low, swampy piece of federal property called Ellis Island was handed over to the Secretary of the Treasury to build the first *federal* immigrant receiving station.

Ellis Island opened on January 1, 1892. This edifice was cavernous: constructed entirely of wood, it was three stories high and had numerous windows for light and air. It was designed to "easily" handle up to ten thousand immigrants a day. In 1891, the federal government had assumed total jurisdiction over immigration affairs at all ports, not just New York, so federal immigrant processing centers were established at other ports as well, among them Locust Point in Baltimore Harbor, Angel Island in San Francisco Bay, and Galveston Island at Galveston.

Just when the United States was poised and ready to take on the onslaught of immigrants, immigration dropped off abruptly as cholera broke out in European ports in August 1892. Then the U.S. economy slipped into a long period of depression that lasted for years.

On June 14, 1897, just before midnight, fire broke out in the all-wooden building on Ellis Island and it burned to the ground. All administrative records for Castle Garden for the period 1855 through 1890 and most records retained from the old Barge Office and Ellis Island for the period 1890 through 1897 were lost. No ship passenger lists were destroyed, for they were kept elsewhere in the custody of what were then called the Bureau of Customs and the Bureau of Immigration.

Following the destruction of the Ellis Island facility, the old Barge Office was reactivated as a processing center. It was used as such for three and a half years while the new Ellis Island building was being erected.

On December 17, 1900, the new building on Ellis Island—constructed of steel, brick and stone, and hoped to be fireproof—opened. But it was too small from the start and would have to be expanded many times. Because immigration figures had been depressed through the 1890s, the new station had been designed to accommodate many fewer immigrants than the old one. Officials thought the peak years of immigration had passed!

What this chronology and historical sketch demonstrate is that thousands of immigrants who arrived in New York never set foot on Ellis Island—not even after the federal receiving center had been established there. Take this into account, therefore, before you say your ancestors arrived at Ellis Island!

When the Immigration Act became law in 1924, requiring visas and providing for the inspection of prospective immigrants at U.S. embassies overseas, Ellis Island lost its primary function. It closed that year as an immigrant receiving station. For thirty years it was used, on and off, as a detention and deportation center. Ellis Island was locked and abandoned on November 29, 1954, and placed on the U.S. government's excess property list.

Despite all of the published and microfilmed passenger lists, the indexes and research aids, the instruction and helpful hints, you may not find the ship that brought your immigrant ancestor to America. Success in this endeavor cannot be guaranteed. As already noted, many of the old lists have been lost or destroyed, and thousands of passenger lists that have survived remain unindexed, making their contents difficult to access.

This manual does not describe every resource available for conducting your search, nor does it explain every possible methodology. The bibliography is selective and representative, not exhaustive. The examples, too, are representative. You must analyze your research problem and find the works most helpful to you. Remember, every immigrant ancestor's story is unique, so every search for an ancestor's ship is unique.

As you search, however, you will gain increasing familiarity with the indexes and the lists. You will become attuned to their peculiarities and you will appreciate their riches. Even if your research path does not lead to your immigrant ancestor's ship, your search itself will be enlightening, for it will lead you to appreciate fully what it means that they came in ships: the Europeans, the Africans, the Asians who arrived in America between 1565 and 1954; the hundreds, the thousands, the millions who came—they came in ships.

SELECT BIBLIOGRAPHY

I. RESEARCH AIDS

Colletta, John P. "The Italian Mayflowers." *Attenzione* 6 (2) (February 1984): 30–33. A brief article explaining how to search ship passenger lists at the National Archives for Italian immigrants.

Eakle, Arlene. "Tracking Immigrant Origins." *The Source: A Guidebook of American Genealogy.* Salt Lake City: Ancestry, 1984. Chapter 15 discusses resources, methods, and overviews each national group's settlement pattern in the U.S.

Morton-Allan Directory of European Passenger Steamship Arrivals at the Port of New York, 1890–1930, and at the Ports of Baltimore, Boston, and Philadelphia, 1904–1926. New York: Immigration Information Bureau, 1931. Reprint. Baltimore: Genealogical Publishing Co., 1979. Dates of arrival for every passenger liner, arranged by steamship line.

National Archives Trust Fund Board. *Guide to Genealogical Research in the National Archives.* Washington, D.C.: NATF, 1983. 2d ed. 1985. Chapter 2, "Passenger Arrival Lists," provides a port-by-port description of the lists and the indexes to them.

_____. *Immigrant and Passenger Arrivals: A Select Catalog of National Archives Microfilm Publications.* Washington, D.C.: NATF, 1983. 2d ed. 1991. A roll-by-roll catalog of microfilmed lists and indexes.

Potter, Constance. "St. Albans Passenger Arrival Records." *Pro-logue: Journal of the National Archives* 22 (1) (Spring 1990): 90–93. Describes National Archives records of immigration across the Canadian border, 1895-1954, and their indexes.

Steuart, Bradley W. *Passenger Ships Arriving in New York Harbor (1820–1850).* Bountiful, Utah: Precision Indexing, 1991. Drawn from National Archives microfilm M1066, *Registers of Vessels Arriving at the Port of New York.* . . .

Tepper, Michael H. *American Passenger Arrival Records: A Guide to the Records of Immigrants Arriving at American Ports by Sail and Steam.* Baltimore: Genealogical Publishing Co., 1988. Upd. and enl. ed. 1993. Thorough overview not only of ship lists but other types of records that provide immigrant arrival information.

II. BIBLIOGRAPHIES OF PUBLISHED SHIP
PASSENGER LISTS

Filby, P. William. *Passenger and Immigration Lists Bibliography, 1538–1900: Being a Guide to Published Lists of Arrivals in the United States and Canada.* 2d ed. Detroit: Gale Research Co., 1988. Most comprehensive list available of ships for which lists have appeared in published literature.

Lancour, Harold, comp. *A Bibliography of Ship Passenger Lists, 1538–1825, Being a Guide to Published Lists of Early Immigrants to North America.* New York: New York Public Library, 1938. 3d ed. rev. and enl. by Richard J. Wolfe, 1963. This work has been incorporated into P. William Filby's *Passenger and Immigration Lists Bibliography, 1538–1900.*

III. INDEXES TO ARRIVAL LISTS

Baca, Leo. *Czech Immigration Passenger Lists.* 4 vols. Richardson, Tex.: published by the compiler, 1983-1991. Czech arrivals at various U.S. ports between about 1847 and 1871; extracted from lists at the National Archives.

Boyer, Carl, ed. *Ship Passenger Lists.* 4 vols. Newhall, Calif.: 1977-80. Indexes numerous published ship lists: vol. 1, National and New England, 1600-1825; vol. 2, New York and New Jersey, 1600-1825; vol. 3, The South, 1538-1825; and vol. 4, Pennsylvania and Delaware, 1641-1825.

Burgert, Annette K. *Eighteenth Century Emigrants from German-Speaking Lands to North America.* Breinigsville, Pa: Pennsylvania German Society, 1983 (vol. 16) and 1985 (vol. 19). Information on German-speaking immigrants from the Northern Kraichgau and Western Palatinate.

Cassady, Michael. *New York Passenger Arrivals, 1849-1868.* Papillion, Nebr.: Nimmo, 1983. Thirty-three selected lists naming about 10,200 persons.

Filby, P. William, with Mary K. Meyer, eds. *Passenger and Immigration Lists Index: A Guide to Published Arrival Records of More Than 1,775,000 Passengers Who Came to the New World between the Sixteenth and the Early Twentieth Centuries.* Detroit: Gale Research Co., 1981-present. Originally three volumes. Supplemental volumes published annually and gathered every few years into "cumulative supplements." Hundreds of thousands of names appearing in published ship lists and other types of arrival records.

Glazier, Ira A., ed. *The Famine Immigrants: Lists of Irish Immigrants Arriving at the Port of New York, 1846-1851.* 6 vols. Baltimore: Genealogical Publishing Co., 1983. Since New York arrivals of 1847-1896 are not indexed at the National Archives, this is a very helpful work.

_____, and P. William Filby, eds. *Germans to America: Lists of Passengers Arriving at U.S. Ports.* Wilmington, Del.: Scholarly Resources, Inc., 1988–present. 28 vols. Ongoing. For 1850–1855, reproduces entire lists of ships with a minimum of eighty-percent German surnames. For 1856–1872, lists German passengers *only* from all ships. Indexed.

_____. *Italians to America: Lists of Passengers Arriving at U.S. Ports, 1880–1899.* 2 vols. Wilmington, Del.: Scholarly Resources, Inc., 1992–present. Ongoing.

Haury, David A., ed. *Index to Mennonite Immigrants on U.S. Passenger Lists, 1872–1904.* North Newton, Kans.: Mennonite Library and Archives, 1986. Nearly fifteen thousand Mennonite passengers, mostly Germans from Russia, in chronological order of ship arrival. Indexed.

McManus, J. *Comal County, Texas, and New Braunfels, Texas, German Immigrant Ships, 1845–1846.* St. Louis: F. T. Ingmire, 1985. Passengers of forty-one ships are enumerated and indexed.

Mitchell, Brian, comp. *Irish Passenger Lists, 1847–1871.* Baltimore: Genealogical Publishing Co., 1988. Lists of passengers sailing from Londonderry to America on ships of the J. & J. Cooke Line and McCorkell Line.

Norlie, Olaf Morgan. *History of the Norwegian People in America.* Minneapolis: Augsburg Publishing House, 1925. Reprint. New York: Haskell House Publishers, 1973. Traces to the sixth generation the descendants of the fifty-two/fifty-three Norwegians (one born at sea) who came in 1825 on the ship *Restaurationen.* Not indexed.

Olsson, Nils William. *Swedish Passenger Arrivals in New York, 1820–1850.* Chicago: Swedish Pioneer Historical Society, 1967. Covers all Swedes for port and period, with additional biographical information for about one-third of them.

_____. *Swedish Passenger Arrivals in U.S. Ports, 1820–1850 (Except New York)*. St. Paul: North Central Publishing Co., 1979.

Owen, Robert Edward, ed. *Luxembourgers in the New World*. 2 vols. Esch-sur-Alzette, Luxembourg: Editions-Reliures Schortgen, 1987. A re-edition based on Nicholas Gonner's *Die Luxemburgen in der Neuen Welt*, published in Dubuque, Iowa, 1889. Names thousands of immigrants and where they settled.

"Passenger Arrivals at Salem and Beverly, Massachusetts, 1798-1800." *New England Historical and Genealogical Register* 106 (1952): 203–209. Transcribes nine original passenger lists found in Record Group 36 at the National Archives.

Prins, Edward. *Dutch and German Ships*. Holland, Mich.: published by the compiler, 1972. Passenger lists of many ships carrying Dutch and German immigrants to Atlantic ports, 1846–1855, especially those who settled the Holland colony in Michigan. No index.

Rasmussen, Louis J. *San Francisco Ship Passenger Lists*. 4 vols. Baltimore: Genealogical Publishing Co., 1978. Original San Francisco arrival lists prior to 1893 were destroyed by fire. Rasmussen "reconstructs" them by using other contemporary sources, 1850–1875.

Rieder, Milton P., and Norma Gaudet Rieder, eds. *New Orleans Ship Lists*. 2 vols. Metairie, La: 1966 and 1968. Indexes New Orleans lists, January 1, 1820, through June 23, 1823, on microfilm at the National Archives.

Rockett, Charles Whitlock. *Some Shipboard Passengers of Captain John Rockett (1828–1841)*. Mission Viejo, Calif.: published by the compiler, 1983. About 1,500 passengers aboard ships from Le Havre to New York. (A portion of at least one list—the *Nile*'s—was missed by the compiler.)

Southern Historical Press. *Ships Passenger Lists, Port of Galveston, Texas, 1846-1871.* Easley, S.C.: Southern Historical Press, 1984.

Strassburger, Ralph Beaver, comp., and William John Hinke, ed. *Pennsylvania German Pioneers: A Publication of the Original Lists of Arrivals in the Port of Philadelphia from 1727 to1808.* 3 vols. Norristown, Pa.: Pennsylvania German Society, 1934. First volume indexes lists of 1727-1784; second contains facsimiles of passenger signatures found in lists of 1727-1775; third indexes lists of 1785-1808.

Swierenga, Robert P., comp. *Dutch Immigrants in U.S. Ship Passenger Manifests, 1820-1880: An Alphabetical Listing by Household Heads and Independent Persons.* 2 vols. Wilmington, Del: Scholarly Research, Inc., 1983. Dutch arrivals taken from lists in the National Archives. Fills gaps in National Archives indexes.

Tepper, Michael H., ed. *Emigrants to Pennsylvania, 1641-1819: A Consolidation of Ship Passenger Lists from the Pennsylvania Magazine of History and Biography.* Baltimore: Genealogical Publishing Co., 1975.

_____. *Immigrants to the Middle Colonies.* Baltimore: Genealogical Publishing Co., 1978.

_____. *New World Immigrants: A Consolidation of Ship Passenger Lists and Associated Data from Periodical Literature.* 2 vols. Baltimore: Genealogical Publishing Co., 1979. Deals with arrivals during the colonial period.

_____. *Passenger Arrivals at the Port of Baltimore, 1820-1834: From Customs Passenger Lists.* Baltimore: Genealogical Publishing Co., 1982. Transcription of portion of a National Archives index.

_____. *Passenger Arrivals at the Port of Philadelphia, 1800–1819: The Philadelphia Baggage Lists.* Baltimore: Genealogical Publishing Co., 1986. Transcription of portion of a National Archives index.

Yoder, Don, ed. *Pennsylvania German Immigrants, 1709–1786: Lists Consolidated from Yearbooks of The Pennsylvania German Folklore Society.* Baltimore: Genealogical Publishing Co., 1980.

Zimmerman, Gary J., and Marion Wolfert, comps. *German Immigrants: Lists of Passengers Bound from Bremen to New York.* 4 vols. Baltimore: Genealogical Publishing Co., 1985–93. Lists of emigrants sailing from Bremen were destroyed. This work "reconstructs" lists of some German passengers on ships from Bremen to New York, 1847–1871, using arrival lists in the National Archives.

IV. INDEXES TO EMIGRATION LISTS

Coldham, Peter Wilson. *Bonded Passengers to America.* 9 vols. Baltimore: Genealogical Publishing Co., 1983–85. Names of thousands of English and Irish criminals sent to the colonies as bonded passengers.

Dobson, David. *Directory of Scottish Settlers in North America, 1625–1825.* 6 vols. Baltimore: Genealogical Publishing Co., 1984. Based on published sources and documents in British archives, names thousands of Scottish emigrants.

Ferguson, Laraine K. "Hamburg, Germany, Gateway to the Ancestral Home." *German Genealogical Digest* 2 (1) (First Quarter 1986): 10–14. Hamburg emigration lists, 1850–1934, and their indexes: what they are, where they are, and how to use them.

Hall, Charles M. *Antwerp Emigration Index*. Salt Lake City: Heritage International, 1986. Lists 5,100 emigrants from Germany, Switzerland, Italy, Belgium, France, and the Netherlands who embarked from Antwerp during 1855.

Register and Guide to the Hamburg Passenger Lists, 1850–1934. Research Paper Series C, no. 30. Salt Lake City: The Genealogical Department of The Church of Jesus Christ of Latter-day Saints. Explains the lists and their indexes, which are available on microfilm in the LDS church Family History Library.

Schenk, Trudy, and Ruth Froelke, comps. *The Wuerttemberg Emigration Index*. 6 vols. Salt Lake City: Ancestry, 1986–93. About 84,000 persons who applied to emigrate from Wüerttemberg, 1750–1900, with intended destination of each.

Schrader-Muggenthaler, Cornelia. *Alsace Emigration Book*. 2 vols. Apollo, Pa: Closson Press, 1989–91. Lists about 21,500 emigrants who left Alsace in the late eighteenth through late nineteenth centuries.

_____. *Baden Emigration Book*. Apollo, Pa: Closson Press, 1992. Lists about seven thousand eighteenth- and nineteenth-century emigrants who came to America from Baden and Alsace.

Smith, Clifford Neal. *Reconstructed Passenger Lists for 1850: Hamburg to Australia, Brazil, Canada, Chile, and the United States*. 4 vols. McNeal, Ariz.: Westland Publications, 1980. "Reconstructed" lists based on Hamburg Emigration Lists.

V. SAILING VESSELS AND STEAMSHIPS

Anuta, Michael J. *Ships of Our Ancestors*. Menominee, Mich: Ships of Our Ancestors, 1983. Photos of 880 ships that brought immigrants to the U.S., 1819–1960. Bibliography on ships and shipbuilding.

Bonsor, N.R.P. *North Atlantic Seaway.* 4 vols. London: T. Stephenson and Sons, 1955. Supplement 1960. Enl. and rev. ed. by Douglas, David and Charles, Vancouver, Canada, 1975. Illustrated history of the passenger services linking the Old World with the New.

Kludas, Arnold. *Great Passenger Ships of the World.* 6 vols. Translated from original German edition of 1972–74 by Charles Hodges. Cambridge, England: Patrick Stephens, 1975. Information and photos of all major passenger ships, arranged chronologically, 1858–1975.

Maxtone-Graham, John. *The Only Way to Cross.* New York: Macmillan Co., 1972. Steamships: their construction, grandeur, and mystique.

Smith, Eugene W. *Passenger Ships of the World.* Boston: George H. Dean Co., 1978. Thumbnail sketches of ships arranged by geographic area in which they operated.

VI. THE IMMIGRANT EXPERIENCE

Carmack, Sharon DeBartolo. *The Ebetino and Vallarelli Family History.* Anundsen Publishing Co., 1990. An excellent example of a turn-of-the-century immigrant family's story.

Guillet, Edwin C. *The Great Migration: The Atlantic Crossing by Sailing Ship Since 1770.* Rev. ed. Toronto: University of Toronto Press, 1963. A vivid account of what the voyage was like. Includes a rich bibliography on the subject.

Handlin, Oscar. *The Uprooted: The Story of the Great Migrations that Made the American People.* New York: Grosset & Dunlap, 1951. Describes the immigrants' encounter with American society: how it affected them and how they adjusted.

_____, ed. *Immigration as a Factor in American History.* Englewood Cliffs, N.J.: Prentice-Hall, Inc., 1959. A slection of readings from many authors. Explores what immigration has meant to America over the years.

Hansen, Marcus Lee. *The Atlantic Migration, 1607–1860.* Rev. ed. Cambridge, Mass.: Harvard University Press, 1951. Describes emigrants leaving their European homelands. Pages 172–198 discuss which ports of embarkation in Europe and which ports of arrival in the United States were used by various national groups in the nineteenth century.

Hinchliff, Helen. "Michael Mumper of Pennsylvania: Reconstructing the Origins and Circumstances of an Immigrant Ancestor." *National Genealogical Society Quarterly* 77 (1) (March 1989): 5–21. A superb account of how to research and write an eighteenth-century immigrant ancestor's story.

Hopkins, Albert A. *The Scientific American Handbook of Travel.* New York: Munn & Co., 1910. Photographs and information about crossing the Atlantic in the early twentieth century: fares, menus, what to pack, etc.

Jones, Hank Z, Jr. *More Palatine Families: Some Immigrants to the Middle Colonies, 1717–1776, and Their European Origins.* San-Diego: the author, 1991. Exemplary research in linking American colonists to their European origins and ancestry. Author has done others.

Kraut, Alan M. *The Huddled Masses: The Immigrant in American Society, 1880–1921.* Arlington Heights, Ill: Harlan Davidson, Inc., 1982. A reevaluation of how immigrant groups adjusted to American society. Challenges stereotypical images of immigrants.

Novotny, Ann. *Strangers at the Door.* Riverside, Conn.: The Chatham Press, 1971. The immigration process at New York's Castle Garden (1855–1890), Barge Office (1890–1891), and Ellis Island (1892–1934).

Wittke, Carl F. *We Who Built America: The Saga of the Immigrant.* Cleveland: Western Reserve University Press, 1964. Superb account of immigration by period and national group. A classic in the field.

Washington-based genealogist John Colletta conducts workshops for the National Archives, teaches courses for the Smithsonian Institution, addresses genealogical, historical, and ethnic organizations from coast to coast, and performs research for clients. He contributed the chart "How to Find Your Immigrant Ancestor's Ship" (following pages) to a permanent exhibit on Ellis Island, and his books and articles about researching American families of continental European origin—his latest book is *Finding Italian Roots: The Complete Guide for Americans*—are noted for their clarity, good humor, wit, and humanity. John Colletta's doctorate from the Catholic University of America is in medieval languages and literatures.

How to Find Your Immigrant Ancestor's Ship

1

You must know your ancestor's:

- Full, Real Name
- Approximate Age at Arrival
- Approximate Date of Arrival

Where you can find this information

- Oral family tradition
- Family documents: passports, letters, Bible in-scriptions, etc.
- Civil and religious records: military service, naturalizations, U.S. censuses, marriages, burials, etc.
- Published genealogies and local histories.

2

1820–1954

If your ancestor arrived between 1820 and 1954, a microfilm copy of the passenger list is probably at the National Archives in Washington, D.C. You will search in the indexes there, or, if necessary, in other indexes.

3

National Archives Indexes

These are compiled by port for U.S. ports on the Atlantic, Pacific, Great Lakes, and Gulf Coast, but they do not cover every year or every port!

- If you know your ancestor's port of entry: Search the index to passenger arrivals for that port.

3

1565–1819

If your ancestor arrived between 1565 and 1819, the passenger list, if it still exists, might be in any archive, museum, courthouse, basement, or attic. But many have been published! You will search in the library in indexes to published lists.

Indexes to Published Lists

If you know the name of your ancestor's ship: Search for that ship in indexes compiled by ship name.

Or

If you do not know the ship: Search for you ancestor in indexes compiled by passenger name.

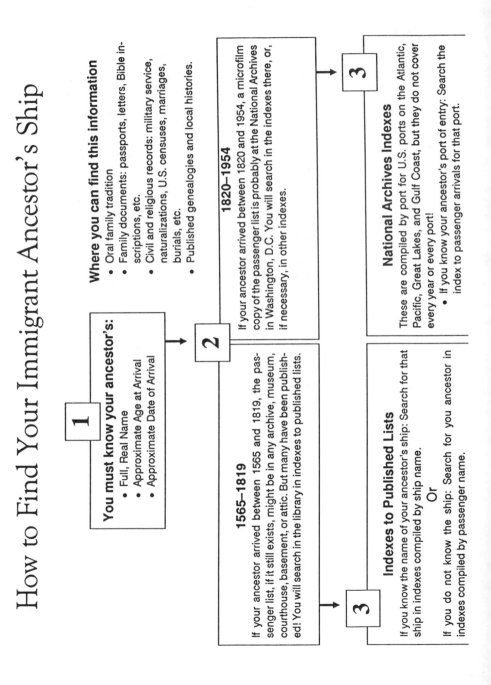

Or

If you know your ancestor's nationality: Search in indexes compiled by nationality.

Or

If you do not know the nationality: Search in indexes compiled by particular group (such as indentured servants or Irish Potato Famine immigrants) or by geographic settlement or port of entry.

Or

If your ancestor was a slave, he or she was not listed by name in the cargo manifest. Circumstancial evidence of your ancestor's ship can be obtained, however, if you know where, when, and by whom the slave was first purchased. Then search

- In the National Archives, manifests of ships importing slaves into the ports of Savannah, Mobile, and New Orleans, 1789–1808.
- In museums, special collections containing manifests of slave ships.
- In libraries, published compilations of documents relating to the slave trade in America.

4

The Passenger List

When you find your ancestor's name or the ship's name in the index, use the reference cited to locate the published or microfilmed list. Then read the list line by line to find the name. Double check what you find against the ancestor's real name, approximate age at arrival, and approximate date of arrival, to be certain you have your ancestor!

- If your ancestor arrived in New York, 1847–1896: Search the registers of vessel arrivals, note which ships arrived when your ancestor did, then search those lists.
- If you do not know the port of entry: Search all available indexes to passenger arrivals.
- National Archives staff will search the indexes if you supply a passenger's name, port of entry, and month and year of arrival. Use NATF Form 81.

Or . . . Published Indexes

These are limited in years covered and specialized in passengers included, but they often complement National Archives indexes.

- Search indexes compiled by nationality or port of entry.

Or . . . The Morton-Allan Directory

This book lists the arrival date for every steamship entering New York, 1890–1930, and Boston, Baltimore, and Philadelphia, 1904–1926, from Europe.

- If you know the name of your ancestor's ship: Note every date when that ship arrived, then search those lists.
- If you know the date when your ancestor arrived: Note which ships arrived on that date, then search those lists.

Or . . . The Hamburg Emigration Index

- If your ancestor emigrated from eastern, northern, or central Europe, he or she may have embarked from Hamburg, Germany. Emigration lists at Hamburg are indexed, 1850–1934. Search microfilm copy of the index at any branch of the LDS Family History Library.

They Came in Ships: A Guide to Finding Your Immigrant Ancestor's Arrival Record by John Philip Colletta, copyright 1993.